Dogs Have Angels Too

Sarah Cavallaro

CUSTOM WORTHY
EDITIONS

This novel is loosely based on Sarah Cavallaro's screenplay, *Keeping Athenia*, a finalist in the MovieBytes Screenwriting Contest, Moondance Film Festival, and Filmmakers International Screenplay Contest.

Edited by Anna Bliss
Cover design by Tony Colletti
Illustration by Eun Lim

Custom Worthy Editions

Custom Worthy Editions are published by Worthy Shorts
The Online Custom Press for Professionals

ISBN: 978-1-935340-86-7
CW100P

For information about eBook or other digital editions that may be available for this title, please visit the Bookshop at www.worthyshorts.com

For more information, visit www.WorthyShorts.com

This book is dedicated to people who wish to redefine their lives by helping animals in need. A percentage of the proceeds from sales of this book will be donated to animal shelter and rescue organizations.

"If the only prayer you ever say in your entire life is 'thank you,' it will be enough."

—**Meister Eckhart**

CHAPTER ONE

It is a blistering, hazy, humid Sunday morning in mid-August. The flowers wilt, half dead and in need of water. For a week it's been like this. Central Park stinks from uncollected garbage. Normally the hyper squirrels jump from branch to branch, but now they simply stretch out in the downward-dog position on thick tree trunks, shaded by leafy branches. Meanwhile, a group of pigeons, some with deformed feet, circle the overflowing cans searching for yesterday's scraps. They peck listlessly at the littered ground, sometimes at breadcrumbs, sometimes at just plain asphalt.

Make up your mind," I say to them. "Are you hungry or not?"

The few people who are around aren't looking to make eye contact. They keep to themselves. I smile at a thin, tired-looking woman in her sixties, with wispy blonde hair and gold-rimmed Jackie O sunglasses perched on her head. She doesn't smile back. Her sheltie, who is groomed like a million dollars, fidgets, squats, then scans around to see if others are observing her vulnerable position. In need of privacy, the sheltie turns her back to my stare.

"I don't have all day," her owner says.

When I owned as many sunglasses as this woman probably does, I always smiled back at others because I wanted to be thought of as friendly and nice. I could have easily gotten away with being bitchy or aloof because I was near the top of the corporate food chain, selling ad space for a trendy fashion magazine, and my clients weren't locals but Fortune 500 movers and shakers. I traveled everywhere in the United States, and more than half the time I flew first class. I loved being the first on the plane and the first off. I also loved the white cotton tablecloths. The last time I flew first class was a few years ago, a month before my company downsized.

● ● ●

Being let go was unexpected. I hadn't done anything wrong. I was working at peak performance, but the company execs claimed they were bleeding money and had to downsize to survive. I felt it was cruel to punish me for their mismanagement, but their verdict was set in stone and I could do nothing about it. Having been successful and loyal was not enough.

It was a humid morning like this when my butch forty-year-old boss with her embossed initials on her sleeve came into my office and shut the door.

"Lena, can we talk?"

"Wait . . . I know what you are going to tell me," I said, holding my hand up to stop her.

"You do?"

"We won the Princess Cosmetic account!"

"Thanks to you."

I was so excited I jumped up from my chair, and she was so somber she sat down. Generally, she was upbeat and gossipy. I knew she wasn't romantically involved with anyone, so it couldn't have been a broken heart.

"Then why are you bummed out?" I asked.

"Because." She leaned on my desk and fiddled with the three small pink crystals I had picked up in a gift shop on a business trip to Sedona, Arizona. I had read that the energy from these beautiful stones vibrated self-love, and although I was a successful career woman, I was no lover of myself. In this regard, I figured, I needed all the help I could get.

"Sit," she said.

"I'm sitting."

"You're standing."

"That's my sitting."

"Seriously, please, I would appreciate your full attention."

I sat down and swirled my white leather chair around a few times. "I really love the smell of leather."

"It becomes you," my boss said. Her words were personal, but her tone was anything but.

"I knew we'd get that account." I remained positive.

Expressionless and matter-of-fact, she said, "We're downsizing and I have many issues to deal with."

"I'm sorry, I'm sure it's a drag. But you'll get through it." I had little compassion for her management problems. I only cared about maintaining my slot of top sales reps year after year.

"We're not just downsizing. We're merging into another company."

"Will I like the company?"

"It's not your choice."

"Do you like the company?"

"They're the same multinational company that is gobbling up all the other fashion magazines."

9

I asked, "But do you think this move is better for us or not?"

"Not for your department."

"Why not?"

Her face hardened and she looked down at her short, stubby, unmanicured fingers.

"There are too many people in the same positions, especially the assistants."

"You're letting go of my assistant?"

"And Jim and Janet and Fran and . . ."

I jumped up and paced around the room. "I don't want to hear anymore. They're getting rid of very good people from a fantastic department. They must be on drugs. I can't work without an assistant. You'll have to talk to them."

"The entire department is finished."

"What do you mean, the entire department?"

"I'm really sorry to be the one to have to tell you how stupid our company has become. Especially because you are our best cheerleader."

"Okay, I can survive without an assistant."

"You won't need to."

"Good, now let's stop talking about this."

"You're being let go as well."

"Me?"

"Yes."

"Impossible. They are not that stupid."

"I'm really sorry."

"They can't do this. They need me."

"They are giving bailout packages to certain executives. You are one of the lucky ones. They'll give you six months' full salary and medical."

"They have no one else like me."

"That's what I told them. But they think they'll find someone."

"They can kiss my ass."

"I'm so sorry."

"You know what? I don't want anything from them. Tell them they can take their money and shove it. I can't wait to see them squirm when I work for their competitor."

"Take the compensation package. You're entitled to it. You have worked here for over twenty-five years."

"I don't want their charity."

"It's yours."

"I'm okay. At least I don't have kids to support like you. You take it."

"I don't need it."

"You lucky dog, you've been stashing it away."

"Not exactly."

"Then why don't you need it?"

"I'm staying."

"You're staying?" I said, half shocked.

"Yes. They asked me."

"Why you? You never sold one account. Granted, you're my boss—but you're a manager, not a creator. Doesn't make sense."

"They had to keep one of us to walk them through the accounts."

"They really are morons."

I had worked closely with this woman, who was my boss by title only, for over ten years. She was a good diplomat with a knack for smoothing over rough personalities. I guess those traits won over sales. I'd confided in her about my failing marriage, and in turn she had revealed her sexual exploits with other women who had worked for her. She loved going down on her twenty-two-year-old secretary, who eventually moved in with her. They adopted two toddlers to fill up the second bedroom. I never told anyone about anything she told me. But now, a lack of compassion in her tone made me feel she had sold us all out.

"I can help you get a job if you'd like. It shouldn't be hard. Your reputation precedes you. So do your good looks. No one would know your age. You look, at max, forty." I'd heard this before; it had nothing to do with her being gay.

I sat down and stared out the window. Drops of rain smudged the glass, and I could see a faint outline of the Empire State Building.

"Nice day out there," I said.

"Typical fucking August," she said.

"It's chilly in here."

I took the light sweater that I kept hung over my chair and wrapped my shoulders. There is no lonelier feeling than to be sitting in a chair that you love that you will never sit in again. "I'll be gone by the end of the day."

"You don't have to. You can stay until the end of the month."

"No, it's better I move on as quickly as possible. Time is essential."

I tried to keep a full smile. My teeth were white and straight, and I'd been told many times my smile was beautiful. I knew it and used it often. She got up to shake my hand. I was wondering why she would want to do that. There was nothing left between us anymore. But I went through the motions and smiled again.

"It's been nice working with you. We'll stay in touch. Let's have lunch soon," I said. But I was thinking, *I hope I never have to call you again. I pray I get a job tomorrow.*

"Let's do that." She walked out of my office and my smile disappeared.

The phones started to ring from people within our company, asking logistical questions about where this and that would go after the merger. I wanted to scream at all of them: *Who cares?* But I couldn't, because some of them had also been axed, so I tried to be helpful instead. Hours passed, then it was lunchtime. I could barely make myself stand up again and face my other coworkers. If I had owned adult diapers, I would have pissed in them to avoid walking down the long, busy hallway to the bathroom. I wasn't sure if I had committed a crime or been falsely accused. Guilty or innocent, the shame of not being enough carried the same noose.

Eventually, I did have to pee, and without saying a word to anyone, I walked through the halls to the lobby and exited the cement monolith in which I had spent most of my adult life. When I got outside and looked back at the gold name adorning the building, I was determined to get even with the company. I ducked into a busy deli and waited in line at the bathroom, behind four other people. After I did my thing, I went home and ate an apple pie, and then I ordered Chinese food. After I gorged myself on that, I went out for a walk and ended up in a bakery, where I ate two chocolate cupcakes with vanilla frosting. Then I went back home and cried myself to sleep.

Later that week, after crying and sleeping for days, I called former coworkers who were also victims of downsizing, I offered words of support, and created vast networking arrangements through lunch dates and dinners. Some of the people I spoke to were excited about their futures and others were depressed. I noticed that it depended largely on age, kid count, and savings. I followed that activity with call after call to other fashion magazine marketing departments. After many fruitless months of breakfast meetings, I widened my net to include home design, furniture design, and art magazines. I was then fifty-seven years old, and the deep recession—which was really a depression, though the government was loathe to admit it—hit the country hard. There were no executive sales jobs in New York City. The bailouts were not meant for the workers, just for some employers. But I maintained high hopes and was still determined to get even by being successful.

One day, however, I felt so desperate that I called my old boss, the one who had promised to help me, but she neither answered nor returned my call. The more she avoided me, the more I called. I called many times and she never called me back.

Between paying my rent, keeping up appearances with nice clothes, regular manicures, waxing, and massages, and taking potential employers to dinner and former coworkers to lunch, I was going broke.

I decided to tap into my 401(k) retirement plan, which I had spent over twenty-five years investing in. The last time I looked, I had about $250,000 in the account, give or take 5 percent. If I took early retirement, I could pay the tax and penalty and still have enough to last until I got a job. While sipping on an espresso at Sant Ambroeus, a trendy Madison Avenue coffee bar, I called my investment company. They told me they had invested in Madoff Securities, which was under investigation for a Ponzi scheme. I called the SEC, every related government organization, and many attorneys, and they all said the same thing: there was no money and I was on a list with others to retrieve whatever the Feds could. Like so many others, I was a victim of securities fraud. All those years of selling and planning were over.

● ● ●

The blonde-haired woman yanks her pink-leashed, panting, overweight sheltie away from the evidence. The dog seems almost ashamed. The woman sees me watching her but apparently doesn't care what I'm thinking or might say to her. She makes no attempt to pick up the dog poop, which has already attracted swarms of buzzing flies.

"Come," she says to her old sheltie.

"Pick it up! It's the law!" I call out to her.

She ignores me, and her dog ignores her.

"Abby, I'm speaking to you." The woman tugs hard on the leash and the dog motors slowly behind.

They walk out of the park's 59th Street exit, past a lineup of costumed men sitting on horse-drawn carriages waiting to snag their first customers. The horses have black leather blinders fastened on the sides of their eyes and manure buckets attached to their behinds. The woman's sheltie barks at a large brown horse, but the horse doesn't move a muscle.

Then, to my surprise, several photojournalists aggressively surround the lady, barking question after question at her. Her sheltie tries to defend her owner, but her whimpers are no match for the feeding frenzy. My curiosity piqued, I walk quickly to the exit to listen in.

"Your husband bilked people of billions of dollars. You worked with him. Where's the money?" says the most aggressive reporter of the bunch.

She doesn't answer and keeps walking. They hustle in front of her. She avoids them and continues.

I approach the aggressive reporter. "Don't scream at older women. It's unbecoming."

His face is flushed with pent-up anger. "You're defending a sociopath."

"A man should never scream at a woman, no matter what. Didn't your mother teach you anything?"

"Lady, you're defending a criminal."

"Let me remind you, we are all innocent until proven guilty."

Inspecting my somewhat worn-out pink pants suit and gray roots, he dismissively says, "Let us get the story, then you read it."

The lady quickly runs across the street. The others follow close behind. There is nothing else I can do, so I walk back into the park.

I've never seen her face before, but that's not surprising since I don't read the newspapers or watch TV anymore. I don't even have a computer. But I'm like that lady in three ways: I keep busy walking dogs in Central Park, I have pink leashes, and I used to emulate Jackie O's style.

By the time I'm crossing the park, I'm chanting a long-overdue prayer of thanks to Dr. Styler for helping me find my volunteer job at the animal control center over a year ago. Without this job, I would never have been able to weather the series of hardships I faced.

* * *

After I lost my job, my period stopped immediately. My body

entered premature menopause and my sex drive disappeared. My husband, who was sometimes employed as an actor and refused to work in any paying job (partly because I enabled his belief that he would be a famous actor one day), started to have affairs with young actresses. He blamed me for going through menopause at the wrong time. He said he was doing what normal men do and that I was acting abnormal. He told me he would stop cheating if I gave him oral sex, but I felt betrayed and refused. His womanizing disgusted me. When I ran through all my money, which also supported him, he left me, saying that I had made him codependent and that he needed to break away and grow. He took his clothes and his acting books and nothing else, not even a photo of us.

Eventually, I lost my beloved river-view apartment on the Upper East Side, where I'd lived with my husband for ten years, and where I'd only recently grown accustomed to living alone. The world came to a temporary end that night when they padlocked my front door. I hadn't paid the rent for over a year. The neighbors were embarrassed and hid in their apartments as if I had committed a crime. I realized I didn't have anyone to call because in all the years I'd lived in New York I hadn't made one good friend. I'd been too busy socializing with my clients and coworkers, and catering to my husband's career needs. Now I was on the street, armed with a low cell-phone battery, twenty-five dollars in cash, maxed-out credit cards, and a half-read romance novel.

I went to a twenty-four-hour coffee shop and watched Mexican deliverymen come and go all night carrying food packages. They hung the plastic bags on the handlebars of their bicycles and rode off, returning many hours later with sweat dripping from their foreheads. When I got tired of watching their struggles, I turned to my trusty romance novel, which became a pleasant habit after my divorce. Normally, reading these novels calmed me down, but the desire to be tucked in my own bed by someone who loved me gnawed deeply at my sense of security. When the sun rose, I said thank you to the waiter and paid for my tea, leaving a bigger tip than I could afford. I walked around the entire day like a zombie. All the buildings looked the same, like nameless, grey stone markers in a cemetery. At nightfall I went to another coffee shop and ordered eggs and toast. I was starving. It took me a minute to finish my meal, and then for the rest of the night I studied all the customers coming in and out. I tried guessing which ones were more like me. This passed the time and kept me awake. In the morning I paid for the food with seven dollars and a tip. I had twelve dollars left.

For a few days, I slipped in and out of coffee shops, ordering a tea at most. I didn't sleep at night, only on park benches during the day. I had nothing left to read except old newspapers people left on benches. On the fourth night I went into a coffee shop and fell asleep at the table. They couldn't wake me. When I awoke, the waitress said they had let me sleep a few hours. They gave me two glasses of canned fruit juice and asked me to leave. The sun wouldn't rise for another two hours, and I was afraid to go to Central Park. I called the city social service department and asked where the nearest shelter was. I went there and fell asleep for what seemed an eternity.

When I awoke, I thought I was in my own bed before realizing the sheets were itchy, the blanket too thin, and the lighting too harsh. My heart raced and seemed to explode in my mouth. I couldn't breathe. I thought I was dying of a heart attack, so the shelter workers rushed me to the hospital. I was treated immediately. It turned out to be a severe anxiety attack. That's when I met Dr. Styler.

Dr. Styler says walking is healthy for a sixty-year-old woman who has high cholesterol and a history of heart disease and stroke in the family. That's a good thing because the animal center is on the Upper East Side and my room is on the Lower East Side. I see her once a month, not because she is an internist, but to chat with her about the kinds of decisions baby-boomer women face. She believes we can feel younger and healthier as we age if we engage in what we enjoy—in terms of work and relationships, but especially our relationships to ourselves.

I lived in a homeless shelter while continuing to search for a job. Now, when I sometimes overhear people complaining about how small their apartment is, I say to them, "Try living in a shelter for a while. You'll kiss the tiles of your own bathroom floor once you do." The shelter was crowded with chronically stressed-out women who had very little hope. Everybody was struggling and isolated and miserable. The feeling of hopelessness was as contagious as the flu that circulated among us a few times. Once, I got so sick that I thought I'd die right there. But I couldn't accept dying in a homeless shelter when I had worked so hard to change my life by moving to New York. I couldn't let a misfortune that I had no control over defeat me. I had to survive the flu and reclaim my dignity. That night, I had sunk so low that I literally had to lie in my own sickness and filth until I asked for help from strangers. It took me about a week to recover.

That entire winter I heard horrific stories of physical and emotional abuse. These women had been betrayed again and again by people who claimed to care about them, starting from their childhoods and ending with the final betrayal—self-rejection. I believe that's where the hopelessness really sets in.

The first place I stayed had about forty beds in a large gymnasium structure. About thirty were occupied. My mattress was thin and I could feel the springs every time I turned over. The bed to my left was vacant, and the one to my right was occupied by a tall, thin, twenty-year-old woman with black hair who could have been a supermodel. I couldn't understand how a woman like her had ended up there. And she couldn't understand the same of me. She cried often, and solicited my friendship. Many nights passed before I allowed a conversation. I didn't believe friends could exist in this desperate place where everyone either prayed or cursed God. I never knew who had just gotten out of prison or for what crime. This striking young woman who slept to my right turned out to be a transsexual who had been providing sexual services to an older man in exchange for a place to live and a warm body to love. She said they'd been together since she was fifteen, and that when he nearly beat her to death, she finally left. She had no money and nowhere else to go. Her paperwork identified her as a man, but when they put her into a shelter for men, she was raped. Finally, an intake social worker who received training on these issues put her into our women's shelter. She told me that women account for half the homeless population and are underrepresented in homeless literature. She aspired to help end homelessness for women, and this gave her strength.

There was a young in-house social worker who demanded a weekly session with me. She said very little of interest to me. I had no use for her inappropriate pep talks: "You can do

it. You can change your life back to what it was. Go for it."
She never listened the way Dr. Styler did, or ever seemed to
understand much about me. She wore a large diamond ring,
and I was surprised that no one hit her in the head and took it.
The gold Cartier pen my boss had given me for Christmas one
year was stolen by someone in the shelter. I wondered if the
social worker took it while I went to use the bathroom during
one of our meetings, because she eyed it many times during our
sessions and asked if the sapphire on the handle was real. But I
didn't dare accuse her because I couldn't risk being thrown out
during the winter.

When spring came, my skin was welted from the harsh
chemicals they used to sanitize the sheets with. I decided I had
to leave. I said good-bye to my only friend, the transsexual,
and kissed her on the cheek. She begged me not to leave her.
I insisted I had to go, for my sanity and health. I told her she
should leave too, because all we were doing in there was rotting.
That angered her and she slammed her head against the bed,
accusing me of deserting her. They wrapped a towel over her
bloody head and took her away to the hospital to get stitches.

I decided it was then or never, so I packed up my meager
belongings and left. I headed to Central Park and sat in deep
solitude, watching people all day. That night I forced myself
to sleep in the park. I waited until sunset, then walked around
waiting for divine intervention. When that didn't come, I found
a bench. I sat for a while and then dozed off. I was awakened
by a group of sadistic, loud-mouthed teens having fun bullying
me to get up. I ran away, thinking they'd kill me, and got lost in
the flowering bushes, where I stayed hidden until morning. I
hated the sounds of insects; their buzzing drove me crazy. But

sleeping there was better than listening to snoring and crying at the shelter. However, the darkness invited people too, not just insects. They did drugs and had sex in these shadowy enclaves of the park. Night after night, some of the same people would return, and soon I realized that the park had a whole subculture of night owls seeking gratification. For a month, I sought shelter behind clusters of trees and inadvertently witnessed many furtive encounters. Fortunately, I never saw a rape or a murder.

In the mornings I'd go to Starbucks to wash up and change into one of my precious interview outfits, which I protected just as I would my last morsel of food. Getting interviews was a feat in itself, and they mostly came from past business relationships. Realizing that my business contacts felt sorry for me scared me more than the interviews themselves. But somehow I kept going, still believing there was a place for me in corporate sales. I searched for executive positions in corporations and nonprofit institutions, but nothing panned out. Then I searched for assistant positions—again, to no avail. I forced myself to take a part-time job selling perfume at Bloomingdales and moved into a hostel. This arrangement only lasted a few months because I found it repulsive to barrage lonely old women scuffling aimlessly down perfume aisles with my fake smiles, telling them, "You smell so young and fresh." They would look at me as if I was insensitive and stupid. When I brought this up to my manager, she told me I was overreacting, and that the customers pretended not to like it but their market research showed that they secretly did. "Research doesn't lie," she'd squeal. "Yes, it does. It depends on the sampling and the hypothesis. In my job at the magazine . . . " But she'd cut me off and tell me that was the past and she wasn't interested in what other companies did. I volunteered to do my own study. She told me I was out of line and fired me.

Down the street I took another job selling women's cashmere sweaters at a small store. They demanded that I tell the customers how great they looked, regardless of the fit. I forced myself to compliment anyone who put on a sweater. Some of the customers accused me of being insincere, but my manager liked me. I thought I'd found a home, but then out of nowhere I was told their lease was up and they couldn't afford the rent increase, so they had to merge with another store and I was not needed anymore.

I had managed to tuck away a small wad of cash but was close to broke again, and part-time work was harder to find than ever because I had let myself get depressed. With what money I had left, I subsisted on stale bread and peanut butter, not many veggies, and no fruit. I had lost two beautiful upper right molars to gum infections. It was painful and somewhat noticeable, but not obviously offensive. However, before long, my front tooth was hanging by a thread. One day I bit into a hard piece of bread that I'd gotten free at a bakery at closing time, and there was blood and a large front tooth sticking out of it. Now my smile was unsightly, and my beautiful interview clothes didn't fit anymore. I started to search in thrift stores for outfits I could wear. My roots were gray because I couldn't afford hair dye or haircuts, and nobody wanted to hire a toothless salesperson.

Dr. Styler said that in order to get back on track I had to make serious changes. I never told her how down and out I really was because I didn't want her handouts. After all, we were both professional women and I took her advise to heart. She said self-reform would have to start with what I said to myself, moment to moment. She insisted I tell myself positive things about my life, regardless of what my world looked like. I scrounged up every positive image I could and held it in my mind's eye. Eventually, I did accept some of her money, promising to pay her back. She also gave me hair dye and paid to have a bridge made for my missing teeth.

Best of all, since she was a large donor to animal causes, she got me a volunteer job at the animal center as well as a dog-walking job that paid twenty dollars an hour. With a queasy feeling in my stomach, I thanked her and didn't mention that I'd had a lifelong fear of dogs. As a little girl, I'd once been badly bitten by a German shepherd, and for years after that I couldn't enter a room if a large dog was there. In fact, in the immediate aftermath, if so much as a poodle snarled, I'd run to the other side of the room. But if necessity is the mother of invention, then it's also the mother of overcoming one's fears. Working at the animal center has proven to be very effective exposure therapy, and I've discovered that, beneath the early negative conditioning, I have a natural affinity for animals, even if large dogs sometimes still frighten me.

The dog-walking job didn't last long because an unexpected problem occurred with a very sweet bulldog who was noticeably small for his breed. He was nicknamed Dwarfy. While on a walk, he accidentally ate rat poison somewhere on the street and died within a few hours of me returning him to his apartment. The owner unfairly accused me of negligence, which stopped me from wanting to walk dogs for a living ever again.

Immediately afterwards, Dr. Styler found me a part-time cleaning job for Dr. Pauly. On the first day, when I was on my hands and knees in Dr. Pauly's bathroom, I found myself crying into the bucket of dirty Mr. Clean solution. I cursed the rat poison, the government, God, my dead parents, my boss, and last but not least, my ex-husband. But then, purged of so many pent-up tears and curses, I began to scrub the shame out of my hell. I learned that there was something almost therapeutic about cleaning an apartment, just focusing on the task at hand.

CHAPTER TWO

When I get within twenty feet of the animal center, a sweet aroma catches me. Half-full containers of sweet-and-sour pork are perched upright in the nearby garbage can. No human I know will ever see me eat this garbage. They'd frown at my choice, but it affords me a full stomach until noon.

As I'm scrubbing my nails clean with sanitary wipes from the barbecue restaurant that I often frequent for leftovers, I hear voices. The female voice is sad and scared, and the male voice is aggressive and salesman-like. I look up to see whom these voices belong to. Standing on the right side of the shelter's front door, leaning against the red brick wall, is a young, thin, very attractive, blond-haired woman. She seems to be using the wall for support. He's pulling a small dog from her arms. With his sleek, black hair and crisp attire, he looks like the young professional type. She could be a senior in high school and he could be a senior in college. The dog yelps and squirms between them.

I take out several frayed pink leashes from my pink faux-leather purse, which I found in a garbage bag on Madison Avenue, keeping my ear to their conversation. What would Dr. Styler say about these young people? Would she recommend that I mind my own business?

The young woman begs, "I can't bear this. Please, I'll do anything you want."

Unfazed by her attempt at reconciliation, he stares at his shoe while kicking some dirt off his heel. "Look, just do it and get it over with." He grabs the dog from her.

The dog growls at him and tries to jump out of his arms back into hers. She decides to calm the poor creature down with lies while petting it softly on its pretty beige-and-white forehead. This dog reminds me of JonBenét Ramsey, the beautiful little girl who was murdered in Colorado by an unknown person. At first they thought her mother murdered her out of jealousy. I think this guy is jealous of his girlfriend's affections for her dog.

"You'll only be here for a day, sweetie. We'll be back later," she coos. For a minute the dog lies sedately in the young woman's arms.

"Why did you adopt her in the first place?" he asks.

"Because she was the runt of the litter and no one else wanted her. She needed me."

"But your father didn't want her in the apartment."

"I thought he'd change his mind."

"Him, never."

They are quiet. Then he slams her with a threat, hoping this technique will put an end to the matter. "If you still want to live with me, she goes or you go back home to your father."

"But you said you'd give her a chance," she murmurs.

"Yeah, if she were trained," he snaps back.

"I promise I won't ask you to buy her food or take her to the vet or do anything for her."

"Do you really think your father will keep giving you money when you're out of his apartment?"

"I'll get a job."

"And you're going to throw away NYU in the fall?"

"If I have to start a year later, I will."

"He might not pay for school if you move in with me."

"I'll figure something out," she says with confidence. I believe one day she will, but before that day comes, she'll be on the path of painful compromise.

He twiddles his jacket and concentrates his gaze into the distance. Whatever he is thinking can't be with her best interests in mind because he is not looking into her sorrowful eyes. If he felt for a moment her torment, he'd smack himself for being so foolish.

"Stepping in her shit this morning and last night is not what we agreed to."

"It was an accident," she defends.

"And the barking?" He imitates a piercing, high-pitched bark.

"She doesn't sound like that."

"Yeah, she's more annoying."

"I can train her."

"Just get it over with."

"Please, please don't make me choose," she begs, grabbing his arm. Clearly, she still feels great affection for him.

"Let go," he orders her.

"I'm the culprit, not her," she responds sweetly.

"This is the right place for her."

"Why?"

"They'll find her a good home."

"Do you really think so?" she asks.

He glares at me because he's noticed that I'm staring at him.

When you feel you have nothing to lose and you don't want anything from the other person, you can pretty much do and say what you want. There's a perverse sense of freedom when you've reached that position, as I have.

"That strange lady in pink keeps staring at us. This city is filled with weirdos."

"And what are you?" I ask.

"For one thing, I'm not a stalker like you," he accuses.

The distraught young woman ignores our exchange. She cries, "My mother did this to me."

"Not the same. This is a dog, not a kid."

"There is no difference." Her high-pitched plea makes the dog jump up trying to escape his iron grip.

"I gave your dog many chances. Now let go of her."

She shakes her head back and forth. "No."

He shouts, "Then get the hell out of my life and don't live with me."

"I can't. I love you."

She releases the terrified creature. He quickly removes the dog tag from the dog's neck and hands it to his girlfriend. She holds it affectionately in her hand. He carries the crying dog through the front glass door of the shelter, my home away from home. I follow behind.

Sheila sees me and smiles that welcoming here-you-are-again smile. Her hair is dyed powder blue today. She has swapped the diamond stud pierced through her upper lip with a gold stud. I don't smile back. She wrinkles her forehead and looks at me questioningly, wondering why I'm so uptight. Normally I smile and say hello. Instead, I stand in the corner and watch as the phone rings and Sheila politely answers.

"Good morning, Animal Care Center." She pauses. "Yes, we adopt." She grabs a notepad and pen. "What's your e-mail address, please?" She writes, then says, "We're located between First and Second Avenue. Yes, I'll e-mail you our address. Thank you for calling." She puts down the phone and for the first time notices the man holding the fearful dog.

The dog tries to jump out of his strong Ivy League arms. Her spittle covers the stitched white cotton of his left sleeve. He looks back to check where I'm standing. I stare at his darting brown eyes. He grips the dog tighter.

"What can I do for you?" Shelia asks.

The phone rings again.

"Excuse me." She picks it up. "Hello, Animal Care Center. Yes, I'll hold." She squeezes the phone between her chin and neck and says to him, "So where were we? Oh yes, I remember, you were going to tell me something, something I haven't heard before."

He looks down at the counter, takes a deep breath, and looks back at her. "You have a no-kill policy here, right?"

Talking to herself, Sheila says, "Why am I holding for someone who's put me on hold?" She hangs up the phone and without a blink states firmly, "No, some of our animals are euthanized if they are not adopted within a specific amount of time or if they have serious behavior problems."

"Oh, I wasn't sure. Well, regardless, we are moving

residences and the building doesn't permit animals."

"Then why move there?"

"Is this an inquisition?" he arrogantly asks, hoping he'll deter any further questioning.

"No."

"I think so."

Sheila sucks some air deep into her lungs. "Your reason for giving up a pet, one that loves you, has to be better than a change of residence. You wouldn't do that to a kid."

"Better here where there's a possibility of a good home than with me, where there is not."

Outside, his girlfriend is crying, but waiting patiently like a trusting child, hoping that her sacrifice will garner his unconditional love. When I was her age, I was equally trusting.

Sheila is disturbed by the young woman crying outside the front door. "Are you sure she wants to get rid of the dog?"

"Like I said, we want a good home for her. Try and find one," he snaps.

"I will do all I can for her . . . as I do for them all."

He places the little dog on the reception counter. She lies down, shaking—and, I notice, leaking urine. Sheila gently takes her into her arms and strokes her until she's calm.

The dog licks Sheila's hand. Sheila smiles. "Is she trained?"

"Yes," he says.

At least he's smart enough to lie. Because the shelter doesn't like to train dogs, and untrained ones are harder to adopt.

"Good girl." Sheila speaks to her as if she's a small child. "So I guess that's all for now?"

"Yes, you can say that," Sheila confirms in her efficient manner.

I decide to block the man's way by standing right in front of the exit. I want him to feel remorse, to think twice, to change his mind, but he politely says, "Excuse me." I move just enough to give him room to squeeze by. When the door opens, the humidity billows in and I follow him out and stand there, listening. The girl's eyes are filling with tears. She can't find a tissue in her leather purse, so she wipes her eyes with her forearm. After he massages the back of her gold-chained neck, he gives me a stare that says, "Leave us alone."

The girl's bloodshot eyes fall to the cracked cement sidewalk filled with old gobs of yesterday's gum. "She must be devastated," she says softly.

"Dogs don't have those types of emotions," he states, as if he has a PhD from Harvard in animal behavior. Having won this battle, he gently takes her arm and leads her away toward First Avenue.

I'm utterly sad. Sad for her, sad for the animal, just plain sad, and I let the sadness run through my body like waves massaging a shoreline, calming down eventually.

When I walk back into the reception area, I'm dripping with sweat. Shelia hugs me and says, "Miss Pink, I've never seen you get involved with the customers like you just did."

"Dear, you don't want to hug me. I'm all sweaty and smelly." More importantly, though I don't say this out loud, I don't particularly like to be hugged.

"So, do you think she'll leave him?" she asks, handing me a glass of water while holding the dog under her arm.

"Sometimes things are better left unsaid. Thank you," I say, taking the glass and emptying it in a few quick gulps. Sheila hands me a tissue. "You're too kind. Thank you." I wipe the slickness from my brow.

"Stay hydrated, Miss Pink. We need you!" Sheila pats me on the back and returns to filling out forms and stuffing them into envelopes.

"That's what they all say, until they don't."

"What do you mean?" Sheila asks.

"Nothing important."

"Tell me."

"No dear, I meant nothing."

"Are you ready for another day in the furnace?" Sheila asks.

"Yes." I take the dog from her arms.

"Bambi," she says.

"Let's not name her that," I say as I rock her back and forth in my arms like a baby.

"I feel like killing all men today, and the day has just started. The air-conditioning guy came in again and screamed at me for not knowing how to adjust the temperature properly. Okay, so what if he's right and I keep it too cold? Does he have to scream like a nutcase? What's it to him, he doesn't pay the bills. Everyone here knows I like it cooler than normal. Those animals prefer it cooler, just as I do."

The phone rings. "Hello, AC&C, can I help you?" Sheila slams the phone down and it falls to the floor. "It's all so useless. I'm useless. I can't wait for this day to end."

"Wait 'til you get to my age. You'll either want to fast-forward and get it all over with, or hit rewind. It all depends on how long you're constipated," I tell her as I pet the little dog's back. She is soft and receptive to my touch.

Sheila laughs. "You have a point."

"It's all relative."

"Yeah, yeah, my suffering doesn't hold a candle to all these animals suffering day in and day out, twenty-four, seven. They hate it in here," Sheila says.

"You do everything to help them."

"Not enough."

"You don't have control over the universe. It's egomaniacal to think like that. Just think one adoption every day."

"We also need to teach people to stop dumping animals," she adds.

"And have the Constitution give them the same rights as humans. Actually, forget it, they'd just murder each other under a human constitution," I say.

"Imagine a day without listening to their cries," she says.

"I didn't realize before I worked here how horrible these animals' lives are."

"People are so screwed up. We think all life is created for our use. The joke will be on us one day," Sheila says.

"The ego, my dear, only wants what it wants. Without compassion, it is a cold-blooded killer with no direction."

"So maybe I'm useless here," Sheila says, looking pale and dejected.

"This little one doesn't think so. She thinks you and I are wonderful," I say, trying to be positive.

"The goddess of beauty, what was her name?" Sheila

suddenly asks, changing her tone.

"Aphrodite," I say.

"That's what we should name her."

"No, let's name her Athena, after the goddess of war."

"Are you sure?" Sheila asks.

"This little one will need an edge, if she's going to survive here," I say.

The mutt nuzzles my ear as if to say something.

"What's that? Oh, you'd prefer Athenia? Yes, I think that suits you even better."

"Athenia, I like that," Sheila says.

Athenia kisses my cheek in approval.

"Her little tongue is soft but she smells like pee," I observe.

"She better be trained!" Sheila says.

"Of course she is." But I'm not sure.

"That jerk who dropped her off had big ears, did you notice? I've never trusted guys with big ears. They have problems listening. Besides Athenia, more dogs came in last night. We can't keep up with them all, they're coming in so fast. I've never seen it like this. It must be the recession. Come, I need your help." She transfers the phone to an answering service and leads the way to the back where the kennels are. Athenia trembles in my arms.

I assure her, "Nothing will happen to you." Her breathing quiets down, but quickens again when we arrive at the kennel area.

The stale, lingering odor always disturbs me, and although the cages are scoured almost daily, there is too much to clean and not enough people to do it. The corridor is lit with long, flickering florescent bulbs that give headaches to people like me, who are sensitive to artificial light, and the walls are painted a dreary hospital-green. Not a happy place, which is why I like to keep the poor creatures in the park as much as possible. Hundreds of cages are filled with cats and dogs of all sizes, breeds, and personalities. They have become prisoners. They've done nothing wrong except be born. They need human contact so desperately that ignoring them is tantamount to beating them.

Athenia, the hyper-sensitive being in my arms, shakes uncontrollably. She's probably used to sleeping in the couple's bed, snuggled up against the girl between satin sheets, amidst their familiar voices and human scents. Now she'll only hear other dogs and cats crying and scratching metal with their paws and banging themselves against the bars. Her shaking grows into convulsions.

"I will not put you in a cage," I promise.

"Can you really promise her that?" Sheila says.

"Yes, if I can get her adopted today."

"Miss Pink, we take a vow of nonattachment, remember? Otherwise, we can't be objective and help them all equally. Those are your words, not mine. I'd kill every animal abuser if it were legal. We need to find a clean cage. Why don't we pair her with this little brown poodle? They weigh about the same. Perhaps they'll be friends."

"Perhaps," I say.

Through the bars, Sheila pets the poodle who acts like a Mexican jumping bean. "Let's see how they get along," she says. She opens the cage and the disfigured miniature poodle jumps up, trying to get into my flabby arms, and growls at

Athenia.

"Miss Pink, she may snap."

"Relax, Brownie. I've brought you a friend," I say.

"Sister, the poodle is so desperate she doesn't care about making a new friend."

"The more we need, the less we get. It's a bitter lesson," I say as I massage the poodle's thin body.

"A poodle isn't capable of learning the way humans do," Sheila says.

Sometimes Sheila can be dense. I decide to share something personal with her, hoping to offer her a new perspective. "What I mean is, we have to get over some of our unmet needs. For instance, I sometimes feel I need my mother, since I lost her at a young age, but I can never get her back, and searching for her in others will only make me miserable. So I've had to become a mother to myself."

"Dogs can't transcend their circumstances," Sheila says.

"I wouldn't underestimate them, or overestimate what people can do. Sure, we invented electricity. We found cures to all types of bacteria. We put men on the moon. You would think we could save these dogs."

The poodle jumps at my face, desperately trying to kiss me. Her breath is bad and I don't like her hyper licking, but I tolerate her kisses because I know she needs to give them.

"The unsociable ones will never have homes," Sheila says.

"We can retrain them."

"That's delusional. We don't have enough staff!"

"Where's Shorty?"

"He was adopted last night."

Smiling, I say, "Precisely my point. He was resocialized. What a little cutie."

"One example out of thousands," she says.

I stop our conversation because we do not agree on this point and we both prefer to avoid conflict.

Athenia rests peacefully in my arms while the poodle continues to growl at her. She doesn't budge until she gets bitten on her ear. I pull her away from the poodle.

"We've got a problem here," Sheila observes. The poodle yelps and yelps, saying in her own way how sorry she is but she can't help herself. I pet her reassuringly, telling her, "It's okay, you made a mistake. We won't hold it against you." But the poodle's anxiety is soaring and she bites hard on my thumb, causing blood to trickle out.

"Damn it, you're so self-destructive," I say to the poodle.

I put her back in the cage and close it. She rushes toward the bars, banging her head full-force and practically knocking herself out. If dogs could talk, I'm certain her story would be similar to that of the transgender woman I met in the shelter. At least dogs don't commit suicide, as my friend did, which I found out months later when I returned to the shelter to visit her.

"And you think she can be retrained?" Sheila asks.

"She didn't mean to bite me. She lost control. Please don't report this. If you do, you know what will happen to her."

Sheila smiles gently, and I know that nothing negative will be reported about Brownie. "The air conditioner is on the brink."

I pet Brownie through the bars until she calmly lies down.

Normally I'd never touch this dog again, but I understand her needs. When I get up from the floor to go, she tries to stop me with a blood-curdling cry. Most of the other dogs join in the symphony of despair, so we stand still for a long time until they quiet down, then we start again on our search for the perfect roommate for Athenia.

Sheila stops in front of a large cage with a gallant black pit bull who has a stitched gash over his right eye. He delights in our attention and wags his withered tail side to side. Sheila shakes her head in disgust and says, "Some creep tied this one up to a pole. Poor thing must have been there for days. Neighbors said they'd called us many times and waited for our dispatcher to pick him up. I don't remember the call, nor does anyone else. He was seriously dehydrated, needed an IV. He tried to chew his leash off and almost succeeded. We're short on volunteers today and I know you don't normally walk large dogs, but would you make an exception?"

I shut my eyes and breathe in deeply. "I have never walked a pit bull before, but there is always a first."

Sheila reassures me with another one of her big smiles. "You can handle it. Just remember, if he gets into a fight, grab his hind legs and have the other owner grab their dog's hind legs and pull them apart. Never, and I repeat *never*, put your hands between the dogs to separate them."

I stare into his eyes. I've become much better with large dogs since I've worked here, but that childhood experience with the German shepherd still lurks in my mind and I still want to run sometimes. Of course, Sheila doesn't know anything about this because I do my best to appear calm.

"Okay. I'll take him and Athenia."

Sheila asks, "How come you never adopted any of them?"

"Because I live in a place that doesn't allow dogs."

"But why did you move there?" Sheila asks.

"That's all I can afford."

"By living there you stopped yourself from adopting the animals that make you happy." She is sincerely concerned.

"Sometimes we do the opposite of what makes us feel good."

"I can understand. I've done the same thing with men," Sheila confides. "The one I want, I push away. The one I don't want, I sleep with. The one that wants me, I find repulsive. I think I'm afraid that connecting with someone, having a normal relationship, will make me disappear."

Athenia's babyish paw touches my arm, as if she's trying to add something to our conversation.

"What are you saying to me, sweetie?" I ask her.

Athenia licks my ear as I put it up to her mouth.

"She says that if I really wanted to own an animal, I would have done so years ago," I inform Sheila. "But you're right, finding them homes is what I like to do."

"Don't you miss human contact?" Sheila asks.

"What are you talking about?"

"You're always alone."

"How do you know that?"

"You don't spend any time with the other volunteers."

Annoyed, I say, "I have a life outside of the center, you know."

"Pardon me, I'm out of line."

I half open the pit bull's cage while holding Athenia. "Oh shit, his teeth *are* big," I mumble, taking in the size of those canines.

"What's wrong?" Sheila asks.

"Oh nothing. I was commenting on how healthy his teeth are."

"Listen, if you're afraid, we can call another volunteer in and she can do an evaluation to see if he's safe to walk."

"No. I can do this."

"You're not obligated."

"I'll decide what obligates me, if you don't mind."

"Yes, of course." Sheila shies away from my sudden intensity and gives me space to negotiate my next move.

The sparkle in the pit bull's eyes tells me he's kind. I open the cage wide and he inches toward my hand in a nonaggressive squirm.

"Treat, please . . ."

"Right away, coming up." Sheila fetches several treats from the cabinet like a well-trained dog.

"Thank you." I place a green one in front of his paw, avoiding his mouth. I wait to see if he'll eat it. He takes a small nibble, then another, and smiles at me. It occurs to me he might make a perfect husband. Slowly he will learn to trust me, and slowly we will learn to trust each other, and I can bet that he'll never turn on me once he commits to my affection.

I put Athenia down and wait for him to come out. He retreats to the cage's corner and waits. Athenia pees.

"Sheila, would you please get me a mop?"

"Big Ears said she was trained. This could present a

problem."

"If I weren't in the middle of a get-to-know-you session with this guy, I'd fetch it myself. Please help me."

"Yes." She pivots around and walks toward the supply closet. The other caged animals start barking again. Sitting on the floor, I wait patiently for him to come out. I even put my open palm in the cage and rest it there. Athenia glues herself to my side.

I whisper to Mr. Bull—that's the name that comes to me—and offer a full admission of my own fear, hoping he won't use it against me, because we are the same. Fear for fear makes us equal. You could never do this with a human. Most people, I've learned, will use your weaknesses to their advantage. We can be so blind, so shortsighted, and for what? A crippled, entitled society filled with lies and violence.

"I'm afraid of you, too, Mr. Bull. You have to earn my trust as much as I have to earn yours. I'll wait until you are ready to trust and accept me as a friend." I'm amazed to hear myself saying these words. I've never said them to anyone else before, let alone to a dog. Never thought I could. "Take me for who I am. Then we can be friends."

Mr. Bull, with his pinkish wet nose, smells my palm and slowly moves toward me. His eyes are bluish-green, and his broad, squat frame makes him resemble a linebacker for the Jets. His raw strength and muscle tone are admirable, and any man would do well to possess that commanding gaze. I see bruises on his shoulder. I stroke him distantly with my index finger, until I'm sure he won't blame me for his plight in life or take a chunk of my hand. He wags his tail and I caress him with five fingers. In my purse are many different sizes of collars and leashes. I have the perfect one for him; it's a bit dirty but he won't notice. When I'm about to leash him up, he jumps on me with enthusiasm. Almost passing out, I take in a deep breath and say:

"Now, now. Stay down, good fellow. No jumping up on others like this. They won't understand it. Remember, they don't feel what you feel. They don't know you are grateful for their attention. You're a big boy, and strong and smart; people have trained some of your brothers and sisters to be attackers. People have these killer images in their heads. Mind you, Mr. Bull, they are more frightened of your jaws than of their own horrible weapons and acts of violence. Don't give those motherfuckers a reason to hurt you."

What on earth did I just say to this dog? Getting to know Mr. Bull gives me a sense of courage and it feels good.

Mr. Bull smells Athenia and they start to play.

Sheila holds a stringy mop in her hand and a bucket of Clorox water in the other. She mops up Athenia's urine, and when she is finished she leans up against the wall.

"If she isn't trained, we have a problem." Her tone, for the first time, reminds me of Nurse Ratched from *One Flew Over the Cuckoo's Nest*.

"She's trained," I say, defending Athenia.

"We need more volunteers," Sheila says.

"I will see you later, my dear. They need to get out of here and have some fun."

Sheila gives me one of her needy hugs. I don't like being hugged by coworkers. I always keep a distance and Sheila always tries to pull me closer so as to confirm her affection for me. I have not tested her affection, nor do I wish to.

"Drink plenty of water, Miss Pink."

"You, too."

"You don't like hugs, do you?"

"That's right."

"Why?"

"Just don't."

"I like hugs from women." Sheila's wide thirty-year-old smile reveals many filled cavities.

"Maybe you are a lesbian," I say, half kidding.

"It's possible. I do have problems with dating men. I always want to be the alfa dog and so do they."

"Two alphas don't make a good marriage, no matter what the gender." I leash Athenia and Mr. Bull.

She smiles with her arms stretched forward and says, "Give me a hug."

"I just said I don't like hugging."

"Are you afraid of being a lesbian too?"

"I'm not afraid of anything anymore."

"You must have really been through the wringer."

"No more than anyone else."

"Whenever you feel like you need a hug, I'm here."

"Yes, I heard you the first time, and I know where to find you."

I turn and lead my charges through the kennel. When we enter the reception area it's loaded with people, and two volunteers are standing at the reception desk trying to do Sheila's job.

Athenia pees right at the entrance.

"Not here, out there." A young woman volunteer walks over. "She's not trained?"

"Obviously, she has a bladder infection. With more experience, you'll know one when you see one too. Would you do me a favor and run a mop over it, please?"

"Where do I find it?" the volunteer asks.

"Try the closet," I suggest.

"Where?"

"Ask Sheila. She'll be here in a second."

Sheila walks into the reception area and the volunteer runs to her. "I forgot where the mop is."

"Over there." Sheila points.

"Also, I forgot, are we allowed to take the animals to a dog run?"

"Not our dogs," Sheila says.

"And where are the poop bags?"

"Over there."

"Oh, and should I try to train them?"

"No. It will confuse them. They are only to be trained by full-time personnel."

Sheila is far more patient with the new volunteers than I could ever be. They are half my age and hopelessly scatterbrained. Why would I want to socialize with them?

CHAPTER THREE

Opening the door to the sauna outdoors is a breath of fresh air for the dogs. Both wag their tails and walk happily with me down First Avenue from 110th Street to 96th Street, then across town to the west side. The streets are packed with slow-paced walkers trying to relax and enjoy a day off. When we get to Central Park, we pick up our pace a bit. There is a slight breeze blowing through the smoky haze that blankets the open fields of cut grass. The parks department is diligent about maintaining the lawns where dogs are not allowed. We cannot cut across on this soft green carpet, so we walk around the large circle on the designated path to the drinking fountain. We wait in line, and when it's our turn, I drink all I can, then fill up my plastic container with water and put it down. The dogs lap it up greedily.

We sit under a tree together. Athenia curls up on the ground by my side, and Mr. Bull lays his big head on my lap next to her. Soon, her little belly is rising and falling peacefully in a deep sleep. I'll let them rest, but soon I need to go to work. With a square of plastic poster board and Magic Markers, I have created an attractive, attention-getting sign that says: THESE DOGS NEED HOMES. PLEASE STOP ME AND ADOPT THEM. I take it out of my pink purse and hang it around my neck.

As we walk I listen to their breath and note their body language. Dogs love to watch movement. They bark at Lance Armstrong types racing each other on multicolored designer bikes. People are tossing Frisbees, and when one lands near us, Mr. Bull tugs on his leash to go fetch it. I pull him back. He's strong and almost gets free. I hate having to use leashes for these dogs when I know they would be happier without them, but if I don't follow the rules, we'll all be in trouble.

I hear a man's voice from behind me. "Look, look. It's that dog lady again. She's always here. Remember last week, honey? We saw her near the zoo with four dogs, or maybe it was five."

A woman's voice replies, "What's the difference, four or five? We don't have to count them, do we?"

"I just wanted to put her in context. Do you remember?"

"Of course I do, I don't have a memory problem," she says testily.

I glance back, but continue to walk ahead. They are in their forties, well dressed, and are holding the hand of a young boy. The child says calmly, "Doggies."

At this, I decide to turn around and approach them. The child reaches in my direction, but his mother pulls him off the walking path onto the grass.

"No, don't talk to strange dogs. They may bite."

"Not this little one, and not this big one either," I say. "Pet them, they're gentle."

The husband says, "They seem nice, but we'll pass, thank you."

"The little one won a contest for her tricks," I inform

48

them.

"Is that so?" he says.

"Yes."

"A circus dog, huh?" His wife tries to smile and appear interested.

"In a way, we all have tricks we use to entertain each other. And we all perform theatrically when we need to," I muse.

The child says to Athenia, "Roll over."

His mother asks him if he learned that command from TV, and he tells her he learned it from his friend's dog sitter.

"Oh, that's a relief. We don't like him watching TV. It makes his ADHD more intense."

"I haven't had a TV in years," I say. "And mind you, I don't miss it, but I hear they have an animal channel." I'm trying to be engaging like I once was, when I needed to charm my clients.

The child whines, "I want doggie."

"Maybe one day," his father appeases.

"Don't encourage him," his wife retorts.

"I want doggie, please, please, please." And the boy starts to cry.

"Focus on something else," she tells her son.

"No!" the boys shouts, suddenly furious. He hurls himself on the patchy, dry grass, digging his nails into the ground.

His parents grab him by his back and pull him up. He hits his mother on her arm and cries, "I hate you!"

"Don't talk that way to your mother."

"I hate you!" he says again, and hits his father on his bare thigh.

"You see, we shouldn't have reduced his dosage," she scolds her husband, holding up her manicured index finger.

"I want doggie. You meanie." The boy rubs his teary eyes with his grimy hands.

"Stop it right now," his mother commands. Then his father picks him up and they hurry away.

Upset by the commotion, my dogs huddle close to each other and to me.

I call after them, "My God, he just wanted to pet the dog! Is that so bad?"

They stop, turn around and stare at me, wondering if they should respond.

I take this opportunity to add, "Your son doesn't want anything different than any other kid. It's not personal. He just wants someone to love, someone who will love him back, simply and unconditionally. And I tell you, that's what these dogs do best." It occurs to me that the boy's emotions have been misunderstood and rejected by his parents, who think they know what's best for him. In this way, he's just like Athenia and Mr. Bull.

"Perhaps we will see you again when we are ready to adopt a pet," the father says. They turn to walk away.

"Take the little one, please."

They keep walking.

"She's brilliant!" I persist. But it comes out as a scream.

A flamboyant roller skater, wearing a pink ballet skirt and white lace-up skates decorated with pom-poms, stops and turns off his boom box.

"Is everything alright?" he asks me.

"Not really, these dogs need a home. But screaming at others is not the answer."

"You have every right, girl. It's because you care. Keep up the good work."

"I like your outfit," I tell him.

Looking at Mr. Bull, he says, "Keep the faith. Their time will come. Does she want a pom-pom on her collar?"

"It's a he."

"Better yet."

"Do you?" I ask Mr. Bull directly. "He says yes."

The man takes one of his yellow pom-poms off his roller skate and loops it through Mr. Bull's collar. Mr. Bull does not bark but drops his head in humility.

"God bless him," the man says somberly.

"Why do you feel sorry for him?"

"Because I've been homeless before."

"God bless you, too," I say.

He smiles and asks, "Are you from New York?" He kind of looks like a hound dog with floppy ears and a battered big nose.

"Yes, and you?"

"I'm visiting."

"From where?" I ask.

"Can I tell you a secret?" For the first time, I notice he has a lisp.

I lean in closer to his chapped lips. "Yes."

Snapping his fingers and shrugging his shoulders, he says, "I'm searching for life on Mars." After that, he waves good-bye and gracefully skates off a distance, then turns around and curtsies.

I run after him, tugging the dogs along with me. "You are a true-blue New Yorker. Only New Yorkers have the courage to wear what they want in public. It's beautiful," I say.

Tears well up in his eyes. "Thank you, Miss Girl."

"And you're so open and honest."

"I'm honored," he says.

I feel compelled to hug him, as I seldom feel with others. He smells like too many sleepless nights. "I'm honored too. Thank you," I say.

Then he skates backward, breaking into a cabaret act, dancing and singing to "I Will Survive."

Now my hands are so sweaty that I can barely hold the leashes. The shaded benches nearby are taken, and we have to walk a ways before I find an empty one under a tree. I can smell fresh paint on the green bench, and there is no pigeon shit on it yet, so it must have been recently applied. I find another clean, shaded bench where a sleeping old man leaves only enough space for one more person, and I gently sit down so as not to disturb him. I feel the filtered sunlight shining through the leaves, burning a hot mark on my knee. I shift just an inch closer to the man's feet where it's better shaded. The man is in a deep sleep. Athenia positions herself in the full shade and Mr. Bull hides under the bench. When I pet Athenia, Mr. Bull wags his tail. He likes when I give her attention. What a gentlemen. She sits quietly, watching my every move.

"Athenia, I know I lied to those people and I don't normally do that. I owe you an apology. I just thought I needed to entertain the kid so they would take you home.

Don't feel bad, you are enough as you are, but you are so smart, it wouldn't hurt to learn a new trick. Okay?" Athenia wags her tail. "I knew you would agree."

The old man wakes up. "Did you say something?"

"I hope I didn't wake you."

"A woman's voice is music to my ears." He shuts his eyes and falls back asleep.

Now the two dogs are sitting in front of me. Motioning with my hand, I instruct Athenia to roll over. "Roll over, girl. Follow my hands. Roll, roll, roll." Athenia finally rolls on her back and stretches her dainty paws toward the blazing sun. "Roll, come on, roll completely over." She does. "Wow, good girl!"

Athenia is so proud she runs in a circle around Mr. Bull, then jumps on his back. He affectionately chews on her ear, spurring her to bark as if she were singing a song. But singing is not her talent.

"Mr. Bull, now it's your turn. Just a little trick to give you a special edge, as they say in show biz." Mr. Bull sits straight up at attention. I try to push his body down, but he is resistant and confused, so I back off. He'd prefer to stand at attention like a good soldier. "Lie down, please." But I don't touch him again.

He lies down. "Now stay . . . good, good . . . now roll over . . . yes, yes, just like that." He stands up immediately after the second roll.

"Mr. Bull, you can't afford to be unentertaining. Now lie down again and stay this time." Someone in his past life trained him well, because he listens and lies down again, this time locking his body into a rollover position. He's beyond brilliant and I'm in great awe of his character. "Bravo, Bravo!"

He still doesn't move. His heavy paws point to the blazing sky.

Two boys carrying skateboards approach us. They look around eleven or twelve, and are wearing elbow and knee pads. Their khaki shorts are muddy, so they must have fallen a lot today. One of them walks up to Mr. Bull, who immediately stands at attention. The other hangs back and watches his friend.

"Is he okay to pet?"

I nod yes. The boy approaches slowly and gently. Mr. Bull allows the boy to pet him on his forehead and wags his tail in response.

The boy understands. "Not all pit bulls bite. It depends on who trains them. Some customers bought pit bulls from our store and wanted them to be guard dogs. This one is cool." He motions for his friend to pet Mr. Bull.

The other boy shakes his head. "No way, dude."

I don't want to sound pretentious like that social worker who stole my pen at the women's shelter, so I choose my words carefully. "If you accept what you fear, like Luke Skywalker did, and take a chance on stepping out of your comfort zone, trust me, afterwards you will feel so good about yourself that you'll want to become a pit bull walker."

"Luke Skywalker?" the timid boy says.

"Dude, he's from *Star Wars*."

"I know, but he wasn't a pit bull walker."

"She means a Jedi. Pet him, dude."

"You sure?" the timid friend asks. His padded knees are

shaking.

I say, "Luke, remember the Force. Do you know what the Force means?"

"God," the bolder boy answers.

I pose my next question: "What is God?"

"Energy," the timid one says.

"My mom says God is in everything that exists."

"You guys are advanced. When I was your age, I thought God was my English teacher."

"My mom is a Buddhist."

"Mine started her own pet store."

The timid one moves next to his friend and ever so lightly, with the tip of his finger, twirls the top of Mr. Bull's ear, which has been chewed in half by another animal. He proudly announces, "Hey, your fur is soft. I think you like me."

"You did it," I tell him.

He looks at me in disbelief, questioning whether he really did pet his biggest fear. He is smiling from ear to ear.

"If you boys want to help me find them homes, I'm at the animal shelter on the Upper East Side. We could use your help."

"I have to ask my mom," the bolder one says.

"Me, too."

"I'm there almost every day," I offer.

"Okay. We have to go now." They abruptly gather their skateboards.

"I thank you for being compassionate to animals."

"Bye." They wave and disappear into a crowd of tourists holding digital cameras and small bottles of water. I wonder if I scared them away by being too friendly.

The old man is still sleeping. From his hand his empty bottle of Mad Dog 20/20 falls and breaks into pieces. Mr. Bull barks.

The man wakes up. "Tell her I'll be there in ten minutes," he says.

"Yes, I'll tell her. And I'm going to get the dogs water. Do you want some?" I ask him.

But he's already sleeping again, this time with his mouth open.

I head to the water fountain with Mr. Bull and Athenia. Again, the line is long. I take out my plastic container and wait. While standing there, I see a stranger walking a slow-moving German shepherd. The man is pulling hard on the collar and the poor dog is choking. I call out, "Hey, you, the collar is too tight! Can't you see you're choking him?" He ignores me. Leaving my spot in line, I instinctively run after him, with Mr. Bull and Athenia in tow. "Hey, I'm talking to you. Stop it right now," I demand.

The stranger tells me to mind my own business.

Mr. Bull growls at him.

"Listen, you pink piece of shit, you should be worried about your own dog. He's dangerous."

Mr. Bull growls again.

"I'm calling the cops," the man threatens. "He'll be taken away. He's a menace to all of us."

At first I want to argue and prove him wrong, but I don't want to put Mr. Bull at risk, so I bite my tongue and decide to get out of there as fast as possible.

We hurry away without bothering to look back. We dart

to another path, then another and another, until I think we are safely away from the stranger and his poor German shepherd. Then I say to Mr. Bull, "You can't react that way. That's what they want you to do—to give them an excuse. Never do that again. Do you hear me?"

Mr. Bull lies down and rolls over. He licks his paws while a yellow-and-black butterfly lands on his nose.

"Self-control will be your savior, my dear."

The dogs are tired now and shuffle along like very old people. We come across a group of people seated in a circle in various yoga positions. Some are in the lotus position, others in downward dog. Mr. Bull and Athenia naturally stretch themselves out too, which makes me laugh. I sit behind one of the young ponytailed men in a lotus position. He motions for me to sit next to him. His chest is bare and he has body odor. The waistband of his loose shorts hangs below his bum, and with the way he's sitting, I can see a part of him I shouldn't. He moves his mat over and we sit side by side. The dogs fall asleep. When the group appears to be finished with their positions, I raise my hand.

"May I speak to you all?"

"Yes," answers the brown-haired woman near me. Her anxious look reminds me of Brownie. I'll need to go easy with her.

"Do you see these gentle beings? They are sad because they are homeless. They need your love. Please, can one of you just take one of these beautiful, deserving creatures home with you?"

The brown-haired woman doesn't respond. Nor does anyone else.

"They are well trained and can even do tricks."

"Where do they live now?" the woman asks in an angry, cynical tone.

"In cages at the animal control center. But they can't stay there forever," I answer calmly, ignoring her tone.

"I don't know what else I can do except give money. Do you need money?" an athletic-looking man offers.

"The shelter does."

"I'll send them a check."

"You can give it to me."

"No, I'd rather not," he says.

"He thinks you'll steal it," the woman informs me.

"Mr. Bull, do you think I'd steal money from you guys?" He licks my face. Athenia joins him.

"Did you ever think about working with humans—or better yet, children?" the brown-haired woman asks me, suddenly aggressive. "There are plenty of unwanted teens you can mentor or adopt. The other day, I told my niece who works for one of those animal agencies that abandoned animals get more funding and compassion than humans. People think humans have control over their lives, but they don't. They need more help than your dogs."

"Humans can take care of themselves."

"Not always. They can be victims, too."

"True, but I've been in both kinds of shelters, and I know that I've always been in a better position to defend myself than any dog left at the pound."

"Clearly, you weren't a victim of Bernie Madoff."

"What do you mean?

"The son of a bitch stole all our money."

"Madoff! Well that's a different story. You're right. You were a victim."

"*Thank you* for understanding," she says with feeling and a sudden change of heart. She grabs my hand, which alarms me. "Let's be friends. I like you."

Embarrassed, I pull my hand away. "Okay, okay, but can you adopt one of the dogs?"

Ignoring my question, she says, "I'm waiting to run into that bastard's wife. You know, the blonde woman. I've been told she walks her mutt around here. I'll kill her when I find her."

"Are you sure it's a mutt?"

"It's some kind of dog, I forgot," she says, uninterested.

"Maybe," I respond.

"Maybe what?"

"Maybe a mutt, maybe not."

She pretends she's shooting a target. "She still lives in her fancy apartment that my 401(k) paid for. And I had to move to a third-floor unrenovated railroad flat from a southern-exposed two bedroom. And at my age, it's just not fair!"

"Does that mean you can't take a dog?"

"A dog? I can barely feed myself!"

"Do you know for sure that his wife helped him steal the money?"

"We all know pillow talk has taken down countries and made women rich."

"But sometimes husbands don't tell their wives everything. Mine didn't."

"You want the whole truth? Well, I'll give it to you straight." She can barely talk, her lips are twitching so much.

"My dear husband died of a heart attack. If it weren't for Madoff, he'd be alive." Steadying her voice, she continues, "I hope someone in prison burns his miniature penis off. You know, he even ripped off his mistress."

"What nerve."

"Now you understand why I know his wife knew everything. Why would a woman stay with a freak like that?"

The yoga instructor interrupts, "Quiet, please." The others in the group are assuming their positions.

"Hang around, we can talk again afterwards," the brown-haired lady says.

"I can't. I'm a very busy woman."

"You one of those fancy executives?"

"Yes," I lie, surprised she thinks I still might be.

"It's nice to be the queen."

"Yes it was—I mean, yes it is."

"I need inspiration," she says.

"Adopt a dog."

My skirt is damp from sitting in the heat and I seem to have absorbed some of this woman's infectious anxiety. As I get up, the dogs refuse to move. They are like a couple of colored rocks. I have to coax them to rise with soft words and soft tugs.

"Stay, we can have a coffee after the session. Capital One bank gives it away. You don't have to be a customer. Each morning, I go to the branch on Broadway and 87th. In the afternoon, I return for an Earl Grey tea with dehydrated milk."

"I can't, but thanks for asking."

"Well, I'm here two days a week. The instructor is nice.

She gives free yoga sessions."

I gaze around at the many people on towels and mats who are enjoying the instructor's kindness.

"See you later," I say.

"You will see me later."

What does she mean by that? Does she intend to come searching for me, or is it just her way of being friendly? By this point, I feel too drained to ask, so I just pull hard on the leashes until the dogs are forced to stand and follow me.

Relieved to get away, I wonder if the brown-haired lady is a little crazy. But then, who wouldn't be, after what Madoff has done? I realize that the blonde woman with the sheltie is in big trouble. Maybe I should warn her to dye her hair red or find another park. On the other hand, why should I protect her? In a way, her husband screwed me over too. Maybe if I confront her I'll get my money back.

My long, purposeful strides soon dwindle into short, lethargic steps, and now all three of us are dragging our feet again. Mercifully, the sun is setting and the air is slightly less stifling. Athenia suddenly yelps and pulls hard in another direction. In the distance, I spot the very pretty blonde girl whose boyfriend forced her to abandon Athenia at the shelter earlier today. She is sitting like a statue on a park bench, gazing out at who knows what. Athenia continues to yelp and to pull against the leash toward her betrayer. I tug back and continue on our way. Athenia is forced to follow and very unhappy about it. I'm not sure whether the girl saw us, but at least we are safe now and nearly out of the park. When we reach the entrance, Athenia stops and whimpers while rocking back and forth like a little baby who has been sitting way too long in her soiled diaper.

"She doesn't want you. You'll find another mommy one day." Those words do not console her, so I pick her up and we continue along on the crowded sidewalk. Mr. Bull remains proudly glued to my side, pacing his every step with mine.

CHAPTER FOUR

I'm so hungry. I haven't eaten since yesterday morning. I have to budget one meal a day, which I sometimes eat at night, sometimes in the morning. I make sure to eat protein twice a week and drink plenty of water. As we approach the hot dog cart, I admire the yellow-and-blue color of the vendor's umbrella. Very cheerful. It reminds me of a celebration, and I like celebrations. I didn't have many when I was a kid, but I had a few before my mother allegedly killed herself.

I still don't believe it was intentional. Not because I'm in denial, but because she was a woman who cared about what she looked like, and why would such a woman allow herself to die wearing pink spongy rollers and a dirty bathrobe?

What I think happened was that she went to the car for a reprieve from one of her many fights with my tyrannical father. She took a Valium, turned on the radio, and fell asleep. It was in the dead of winter, so she turned the car on for heat. My father was a heavy sleeper, so he didn't hear the car running until he awoke in the morning and went downstairs. He found her head propped up against the window and all the car doors locked. He managed to unlock one with a clothes hanger. I remember I had just awoken and was coming downstairs when I found him carrying her to the living room couch. Thinking she was just sleeping, I went over and gave her a kiss good morning. She didn't wake up. He tried to revive her, then called 911. I lay in her arms until the paramedics came and pried me away. My father and I had never been close to begin with, but we hardly exchanged a word after that. We simply drifted apart, and by the time I moved to New York City, whatever ties we had left were broken off for good.

I like the way the grease moves on top of the yellow water as the vendor stabs the hot dogs one by one with his long stainless-steel fork and tucks them into soft, beige buns. My dogs wiggle their noses and sit at attention, waiting for a piece to miss the mouth of a messy eater. The vendor has guitar music playing from a boom box. It sounds kind of Middle Eastern. One could belly dance to it, if one knew how.

The vendor asks me if I want anything. I nod yes and fumble through my worn-out pink wallet. I count my change but I'm short by eighty-five cents. A sympathetic bystander with mustard on his lip and sauerkraut on his T-shirt takes out five dollars from his pants pocket and hands it to me. I have not asked this man for a penny.

"No thanks, I get paid tonight."

"Take, take," he insists, thrusting the money toward me.

"No, thank you, but I appreciate the gesture. You're very kind."

"Think of the dogs."

"They are vegetarians," I tell him.

"For moral or health reasons?" he asks.

"Both. Good day, sir," I say and walk away.

Of course, Mr. Bull and Athenia protest with whimpers and backward glances at the hot dog cart, but they soon give up the fight and we continue toward my destination, which is an Art Deco building on Central Park West, at the corner of Sixth Avenue and West 59th Street. The sun has set and the white-gloved doorman greets me, as always, with a full smile.

"Hello, Miss Pink. As usual, you have new friends."

"Yes, I met these lovelies this morning."

"The keys are here."

"Dr. Pauly moved them?"

The doorman gives me the keys. "He's out of town and he left a letter for you." He hands me a small, white, sealed envelope.

I start to open it, but then I put it in my pocket. "A letter?"

"That's all he said."

"Work needs to be done first. There is a time for everything, and I'm not sure why Dr. Pauly would write me a letter when he never has before. I hope he is okay. But I'll find out after I clean."

The doorman half listens, then hurries to the street to open a taxi door for a tenant.

As I ride up in the elevator with Athenia and Mr. Bull, the glimmering brass panel on the floor indicator reminds me of the office buildings I used to visit when selling ad space for the fashion magazine. This building has only ten floors, but those others were some of the tallest towers in the world. In a way, I do the same thing now as I did then: persist and persevere in my work, no matter what, until my time is up. I often joked to those ad people that I was like a postman—rain or shine, sleet or snow, nothing short of calamity could keep me away. When I left my father's home at eighteen to attend college, I vowed to be independent and successful. I vowed this again when I graduated and got my sales job at the magazine. And I vowed this a third time when I found myself without husband or home.

Outside Dr. Pauly's office, I tell the dogs to stay in the hallway and I tie them to a railing. Then I unlock the two locks on his door and enter. The small waiting area has a polished black-and-white marble floor with two brown chairs sitting side by side. Dr. Pauly is considered to be an important psychiatrist. I know this from articles I've read, which are framed alongside his Harvard diplomas. I notice all of these framed documents are hanging crooked on the wall. He must have accidentally bumped them. I immediately straighten them, fluff up the sofa cushions, Windex all the glass surfaces, clean the toilet, vacuum his oriental rug, dust his books, and after three hours have passed I'm finished. There are seventy dollars on the side table where he always leaves it. I think about the hot dog I couldn't afford earlier, hoping it's not too late to find a vendor.

I lock the doors, go downstairs, and return the keys to the doorman.

"May I sit here and read the letter?"

"Yes, of course," the doorman says.

I open my purse and look for my eyeglasses. They are not there. I must have left them in my room.

"Please sir, I don't have my glasses with me. Would you be so kind and read Dr. Pauly's letter?"

The doorman says, "I don't see why not."

"Thank you."

He reads:

> *Dear Ms. Pink,*
>
> *I will be out of town indefinitely and will not need your services at this time. When I return I will seek you again in the park and will reestablish your work routine. I hope this will not cause you discomfort in any way. You are an excellent and most respected worker. I wish you good fortune with your dog crusades. You are living a worthy and just cause.*
>
> *Fondly yours,*
>
> *Dr. Pauly*

The doorman reluctantly hands me back the letter with a sad look. I fold it neatly with the seventy dollars in my pink purse and take a deep breath. I feel like I'm going to faint. Sensing something is wrong, the dogs gather close and lean on my legs. I pet their heads and thank God for their affections. I check the envelope again and realize there is no extra money in it.

"I guess cleaning ladies don't get severance packages," I say.

"Will you be alright?" he asks sweetly.

A familiar twinge of panic runs through my nervous system. Dr. Pauly should have had the decency to give me a month's severance. I tell the unionized doorman something I read in a Marianne Williamson self-help book, words I don't quite understand yet but find comforting: "God never gives us more than we can handle. One door closes, another opens. Having faith makes me alright, my dear. Good evening, sir, and thank you."

"You're a wise woman," the doorman offers, obviously not knowing what else to say.

I will not tell Dr. Styler what happened. She has helped me so much already.

Meanwhile, I don't know where my next dollar will be coming from. When I moved to New York City from Ohio in the seventies, I had dreams of making it, and I did. For a while. Now here I am, practically back where I began at the age of twenty-one. What is the lesson I need to learn? If I don't learn it, what else will happen? And if I do learn it, what will happen?

"Do you know of other cleaning jobs in the building?" I ask the doorman.

"No. I'm sorry. But pass by the building in a few weeks, you never know."

"What about your wife, does she need someone?" I say, only half serious.

"No. She is self-sufficient. Be well. Good luck."

"Yes, good luck is always helpful."

"Good health, too," he adds.

"Thank you," I say.

If I had known then what I know now, I would have eaten my pride and taken the severance package from the magazine. But even that wouldn't have been enough. Maybe if I had spent less and invested more wisely, I would have been able to weather this storm. But then again, how was I to know we'd hit a recession? I've never been big on saving, because, to me, the great privilege of earning money is to spend it, and this is at the heart of the American dream. During my magazine days, it was a powerful feeling to be able to buy whatever I wanted. One time, I splurged on a gold-sequined St. John pants suit in the designer section at Bloomingdale's. It mattered little that the suit was uncharacteristically loud for my life as a marketing executive or that I'd never find the occasion to wear it. When I handed my credit card to the sales girl, I felt proud, light years away from my mother's financial dependence on my father. I've often thought how that dependence, perhaps more than the carbon monoxide in the garage, must have suffocated her.

As the doorman assists someone getting out of the elevator, I turn to my friends.

"Athenia, did you know that every thought I have seems to go around in circles, getting me nowhere?"

She wags her tail.

"I knew you'd understand."

When I leave the building, Central Park West is packed with people. I see a vendor across the street talking to a carriage driver. He looks like he's ready to close up shop. I'm blocked in by a group of tourists asking a woman in a kelly-green designer suit a question. She's walking a standard well-groomed poodle and doesn't care where she stops to accommodate them.

"Excuse me. I need to get by," I say to her.

Her poodle growls at Athenia. Mr. Bull growls back.

She turns away from the tourists and they leave. "Did your black dog just bark at my Lola?"

"He was defending his friend."

"He's too aggressive. Walking him here should be illegal."

"Because he's black?"

"Don't pull that racist card on me. You know, your dog will bite a child one day and they will put *you*—not him—in jail."

I say, "He's already in jail, and he hasn't touched a flee."

She changes her tune. "What do you mean?"

"He'll return to a cage tonight if he's not adopted. You want him?"

"No. He'll get my Lola pregnant."

"Then I really must be going."

But the woman and her poodle want to talk more. "Where are you going?" Her poodle start to growl.

I don't have time for this spoiled woman. "Your poodle needs Prozac, and perhaps so do you."

She smiles in the way a masochist does when getting knocked around. "Now you're talking. You want to go for a drink?"

"I don't drink!"

"Then I'll toast to the two of us," she says as I hurry away from her.

The hot dog man gets his last order of the day. Four hot dogs. One for me, one for Athenia, and two for Mr. Bull.

I'm not sure how late it is, but there are fewer people on the streets and the traffic has thinned out. A slight breeze is starting to pick up by the time we get back to the animal control center. I pull on the front door, but it's locked. Normally I make it back before that happens. I knock on the door. No one answers. I knock again, praying someone is still there.

"What do you think we should do?" I ask the dogs. They

wag their tails with no cares in the world. Just like children. I ask them, "How about a matzo ball soup at the Second Avenue Deli?" They jump up on their hind legs. "Just kidding. But when I have more money, the sky's the limit."

I knock several more times, but it's futile. The dogs are now anxiously running in circles, very upset that I'm slamming on the door. "Sheila will be angry at us," I say. They bark. "Okay, okay, you're right, mistakes happen. Well then, let's look on the bright side. You're in luck because we're spending the night together." I use a motherly tone so they feel secure, but I'm suddenly worried about everything. I have no paying job, Sheila will be angry for not returning Athenia and Mr. Bull to the shelter, and the rooming house doesn't take dogs.

CHAPTER FIVE

Holding both dogs by their leashes, I stand across from my rooming house and survey the building. I wait until the lobby is clear and the attendant has gone to the bathroom. I quickly walk in and head to the stairwell. I walk up three flights, and when I open the hall door, I carefully look around to see if the coast is clear. When I see no one, I run with the dogs to my door, jiggle my loose lock, and enter my pink sanctuary. The walls are painted pink, the bed has pink sheets, and pink curtains hang on the small windows. My rug is pink and white, and so is my blanket. On the pink countertop I keep a hot plate, which I picked up at the Salvation Army. Some might consider this room dingy, but I've created a livable environment, and it is home for now.

"Welcome," I say, ushering in my new friends.

I fill up a bowl of water from the sink and place it on the floor. They slurp together.

"Shhh . . . quietly, sweeties."

A loud bang on the wall makes all three of us jump. Mr. Bull barks.

"Shhh, it doesn't matter, let it go."

Another bang. Mr. Bull barks again, and Athenia joins in.

We hear through the thin layer of Sheetrock a woman screaming, "That's it, I'm leaving! You're drunk again!"

There is silence, then the screeching starts again. "You promised, you liar!"

Mr. Bull barks aggressively and doesn't stop.

There's a knock on my door. I ignore it.

Another knock.

"Yes, who is it?"

"You know very well who it is."

"Oh, Madeline, I'm so glad it's you and not that animal from next door. Be a dear and call the police."

"Do I hear an animal?"

"Yes, next door."

"Not that two-legged one."

"Is there any other kind?"

"Open the door."

"I'm not dressed."

"Open."

"Really, I'm not feeling well, dear. I'm in bed. We can talk in the morning."

Another knock slams against the door. Mr. Bull growls.

"Madeline, he's killing her in there. Call the police."

"If you don't open right now, I'll kick it down and you'll be the one the police talk to."

"Alright, if you insist." I unlock the door and tell Mr. Bull to sit. Athenia is on my bed, sleeping soundly on my pillow.

Madeline is a wrinkled seventy-year-old prune in a flowered housedress. She stands with her elbows out and her hands clutching her waist. "You seem fine. Not sick at all."

Mr. Bull barks.

"Shut up," she says to him, then turns back to me. "And

the roommates?"

"They're here for one night only."

"No, not even an hour. I told you, no dogs. Again, this is a no-pet establishment. I don't like their smells. Never have, and you know that."

"One night. That is all," I plead.

"You take me for a fool. I'm no fool, believe me. For weeks I didn't take rent from you, to help you out. And it's dog story after dog story. Tomorrow, pack up."

"Calm down, dear. I'm only dog sitting."

"That's what you said last time, and I'm not your dear. And also, before you forget again, pay me what you owe me. I'm tired of making all kinds of concessions for you when I don't do it for the others. Nobody would do what I do for you but me."

She doesn't give me another chance to say anything before she slams my door. Mr. Bull howls. Athenia wakes up, looks around, and drops her head back on the pillow. I take my suitcase from the corner and survey my belongings. There isn't much left. Over the years I've sold almost everything. I can't bring myself to pack the little I have. I've created a home here, and now of all times I'm being thrown out. I have nowhere to go. I'm tired. *If you're there, God, please show me the way.* I need help. I actually get down on my knees to pray. The dogs take this as a cue to nuzzle me and lick my face. I let them, silently rocking back and forth like a davening Jew, praying and praying, begging for some kind of intervention.

I say to the ceiling, "What are you trying to tell me? What don't I get?" The dogs jump up against me. "Get down. I'm

75

not talking to you."

We hear another vicious slam on the wall. Not the kind of intervention I was seeking. I walk out in the hallway. Mr. Bull tries to follow me, but I stop him. I knock on the drunk's door. He opens it, holding an empty gin bottle.

"Drink yourself to death," I hiss, blaming him for causing my domestic demise.

"I'm trying," he says, smiling.

I have nothing more to say, so I return to my room and lock my door. The three of us fall asleep in each other's arms.

● ● ●

The morning arrives as always with its screeching buses and garbage trucks and people chattering away under my open window. It feels like it's a hundred degrees inside. I wash up and put out a bowl of water for the dogs. I put on a pink-and-white cotton dress that I picked up at Salvation Army. It's a tad big now because I have lost weight, so I cinch a belt around my waist. I comb my hair in a tight bun and apply light pink lipstick. As we walk down the stairs, I see Madeline sitting in her old chair smoking a woman's cigar.

In her raspy voice she asks, "Where's your suitcase?"

"Upstairs."

"I asked you to leave."

"But I have nowhere to go."

"Try a homeless shelter."

"One day you'll get yours," I say.

I go back upstairs with the dogs and neatly pack my few belongings: several undergarments, three pairs of socks, two cotton dresses, two pants suits, a wool coat, a rain poncho, a bath towel, a set of bed sheets, a blanket, and a thin bathrobe. I am unemotional about it, disconnected. Maybe the stress of losing another home is too much for my brain to process right now. I'm in an altered state. I'm so low I can't go any lower, and the effect is numbing. I've never experienced this before, not even during my time at the homeless shelter.

I carry my suitcase to the lobby. Madeline is still wearing the same crumpled, frumpy housedress she wore last night. I pity her lack of style. Before I go to sleep at night, I iron my clothes by placing them in between the mattress and box spring. I keep my clothes clean and presentable, and they are always stylish. I know which thrift stores carry gently used designer clothes. If buttons are missing on a jacket or a pair of pants, I can always go to the Salvation Army and pick out a few from their huge selection. I have learned to sew, and I carry a small sewing kit with me at all times. If I like a dress but its hem is ruined, I cut it in half and wear it as a top, tucking it into a skirt or a pair of slacks. I banish stale smells by putting the clothes in plastic bags with a little bit of baking soda.

"You could apply for welfare. We accept it here."

"I don't want the state to support me. I can take care of myself."

"The problem with you is you think you are too good for the rest of us."

I hand her half of what Dr. Pauly paid me.

"Here, take this. Don't ever accuse me again of not paying my dues."

She counts the cash. "It's not enough. You still owe me."

"Yes, I know, and I'll bring it by as soon as I get another job. I was laid off yesterday."

"I'll be waiting," she says.

I pick up my pink suitcase and march out of the lobby, the two dogs following blindly, unconcerned about where we will sleep tonight. As long as they are in the company of a caring person, far away from their cages, they are happy.

Every so often I have to stop to readjust my sneakers, and each time I do, Athenia sits and refuses to get back up. I have to pick her up in my arms. My sneakers are beginning to tear apart at the sides. I pray to the sneaker gods that they last until I can afford a similar pair.

I do not like sleeping in the park at night, among the insects. But I have grown fond of the lightning bugs that come out this time of year, and I will do what I have to do until I get settled again.

CHAPTER SIX

Standing in the reception area waiting for Sheila to get off the phone is uncomfortable because I know she's upset with me.

"Hold a minute." She turns to me. "Why didn't you bring back the dogs last night?" She doesn't wait for me to answer. "You know, Miss Pink, you worried me and I don't like that."

"I've never been late before, and when I got here you guys had just closed. I didn't realize carrying Athenia would slow me down so much. I'm sorry."

"Why did you carry her?"

"Her paws were sore from the hot asphalt."

"Is she okay?"

"Yes."

Sheila looks at my suitcase and tells the person who is holding to call back.

"Are you going out of town?"

"No, moving."

"Why?"

"I decided I want to live in a building that allows dogs."

She starts to twirl her frayed hair into ringlets, which means she's tired. "Excuse me a minute." She picks up the ringing phone and says, "Yes, come in, we're open daily." She twirls and twirls as she impatiently listens to the voice on the other end of the line. "Yes, we have kittens." She looks at me. "Yes, we have small trained dogs. Yes, they are good with children. Thank you." She hangs up the phone.

"As I was saying, Miss Pink, even though you did the right thing, you know the rules here, and management is strict with volunteers. You could get into trouble."

"Yes, I know."

The phone rings again.

"Excuse me." Sheila grabs the phone. "Yes, yes, we pick them up. How large?" She listens. "Sixty pounds? Okay. What is your address?" She listens and writes. "As soon as we can, we'll be there. Is it your dog?" She listens. "What a shame . . . what a shame. " She slams the phone down. "Asshole is getting rid of his dog. I can't take this much longer. Have you eaten?"

"No"

"Have they?" She looks at the hungry creatures.

"No."

"Why didn't you feed them?"

I'm broke, I should tell her, but I don't. "I did last night."

"They must be starving."

"Not completely. I found some old steak bones in the garbage. They nibbled but there wasn't enough meat to make a meal for two. Thankfully, Athenia eats like a bird."

"You know where the dog food is, on the right side toward the first row of cages. Go back there. I can't now. There's no one to cover for me today. I just got a memo that they've cut the budget even more. They let go of two employees."

"I hope the killing vet was one of them."

"They need him."

"No, they don't."

"I mean management does."

I'm disgusted with their concentration camp tactics and I want to scream at the injustice, but what good would it do? All I can do is walk back to the kennels and try to help the other dogs. Meanwhile, Athenia and Mr. Bull refuse to follow me and begin to cry. I can't leave them in the reception area unattended because Sheila is about to explode with frustration, so I try to cajole them into following me. They refuse and I drag them by their collars.

The stench is strong today. The two volunteers can't keep up with the demand. I hide my suitcase behind some large food cartons. The volunteers smile at me as they groom dogs and clean cages. The caged dogs whimper as if suffocating, and my two companions are shaking with fear. I feed Mr. Bull and Athenia right there. The volunteer whom I secretly refer to as "overzealous" approaches me. She must be in her early twenties and is wearing tight blue jeans and high heels.

"It's not fair to feed the dogs in front of the others," she says.

"If you intend to walk them, you'll have to change your shoes."

"Today I'm on grooming duty."

"Then don't worry about me feeding them."

"Where did those dogs come from?" she asks.

"From here. I'm trying to find them homes."

"You better find 'em fast. They're doing selections today."

"Who's next?" I ask.

"Those dogs over there." She points to a small dog

running in circles and to a mutt who appears to be a mix of pit bull and lab.

A distinguished-looking, grey-haired vet in a white coat walks in carrying six syringes with long needles.

"How far in does one of those needles have to be inserted?" I ask.

"I was told it's not painful and it's very fast," the young volunteer responds for him.

"Capo."

"What's that?"

Apparently, this young woman never learned about Nazi culture. These animals are doomed, but I decide not to argue with her.

"Let's get out of here," I say to my compatriots as I pull at their leashes. Mr. Bull growls because he's not finished eating. The vet looks over at him. I pick up the remaining dry dog food and dump it into a container in my purse. Mr. Bull jumps up and bites my purse strap. He locks it in his teeth.

"Oh, you're so playful," I say loudly so the vet will hear.

He growls again and refuses to let go of my strap. His tugging is tearing it in half.

"Drop it now!" I command.

The volunteer asks me in a prickly tone, "Is he crazy?"

"No more than you or I."

The vet saunters over and asks me as if he were the judge of all dogs, "Is there a problem?"

Trying to be diplomatic, I say in a very calm manner, "Not at all. No one likes to be interrupted while they are eating, especially when they are hungry. Don't you agree?"

My mouth is suddenly parched, but I can't stop speaking. "With all your education, can't you come up with a better way to deal with overpopulation and lack of love?"

The vet doesn't respond with words but with a wry shake of his head. The overzealous volunteer asks me if I need assistance walking the dogs, adding that she has experience with difficult dogs and the pit bull appears very difficult. I tell her he is not difficult. "We'll see," the volunteer replies, and frowns at Mr. Bull.

"If you want to stay young forever, try smiling," I tell her.

I scoot out to the reception area and advise Sheila to keep an eye on the overzealous volunteer, who always fixates on the potentially negative aspects of the dogs. Sheila half listens as she sharpens a bunch of pencils, one after the other.

"We need the volunteers," she states matter-of-factly.

"That one you don't," I say.

"There is too much work to do here and she has a talent for picking out characteristics that make dogs unadoptable."

"She's prejudiced and jumps quickly to conclusions."

"I'm training her to be my assistant. I need someone who will help the vet do selects."

"Stop selects!"

"It's government policy. I don't make the rules."

"Stop selects!" I repeat.

Ignoring my protest, Sheila asks, "Are they fed?"

"Yes."

"Make sure to bring them back tonight."

"Absolutely."

She moves in for a conciliatory hug. I shy away.

"Oh, Miss Pink, I'm not going to bite you!"

"I would hope not."

I force myself to give her a quick little hug because my general dislike of hugs has very little to do with her. It's just that I've learned the hard way not to get too familiar with coworkers, because then, before I know it, I'll be trusting them as close friends and confiding in them, and expecting them to love me unconditionally. But only dogs seem to have the ability to love unconditionally. It's better for me to maintain a professional distance.

CHAPTER SEVEN

I surrender to the streets with Athenia and Mr. Bull. Today I have a different focus: to find a part-time job. Any job will do. I have given up on trying to find jobs in marketing.

I briskly walk across town and then all the way down First Avenue until I get to the Lower East Side, where I remember passing a few HELP WANTED signs posted on shop windows last week. By this time, the dogs are panting and I need to go to the bathroom. It's around noon, the sun is in full throttle, and the sidewalk cafés are filled with customers. As I tie my dogs to a parking meter under a tree next to a packed outdoor café, a redheaded woman blows a kiss to my dogs. She sips chilled white wine with another woman who has short, dusty-blonde hair and is wearing a low-cut black cotton dress. They seem to be celebrating something. The blonde is bobbing her head, leading their conversation in an excited, high-pitched tone.

"You're finally making a profit after two years of owning the shop. It's the new suppliers I made aggressive deals with. It's all about buying low and selling high. And, of course, supply and demand."

"Sally, you are not buying from puppy farms, are you?" the redhead asks.

"Why would you think that?"

"I have to ask because the profits are fantastic."

I pretend to be fixing the dogs' collars so I can eavesdrop on the rest of this conversation. The dogs are quiet and happy to rest there like tired construction workers under the piss-stained tree.

"But Barbara, just so you know, the new puppy farms aren't like the old ones. They are cleaner and the animals are treated humanely."

"Sally, they overbreed, and some still sell their animals to experimental labs. The thought makes me sick," the redhead says. She wipes her forehead with a napkin and looks at the beige powder stain in disgust.

"Buy Dior. It's waterproof," Sally advises.

"I can't afford it."

"Now you can."

"I'm so relieved you're managing the shop for me now. I didn't know what else to do other than go bankrupt, and I couldn't do that because I personally signed for the lease. I shouldn't have opened the shop without knowing more about the business. But I love animals so much, and my son loves them too. I thought it would bring us closer together."

"The shop will only do better and better. But I have to get rid of that lame duck of a sales girl. She's useless."

"Do what you have to do. You know I trust your judgment."

"Here's to positive cash flow," Sally says as she picks up her wine glass.

They clink glasses.

They will need a sales girl. Follow the money, I tell myself.

I head for the patio so I can say hello to the women. The waitress stops me.

"The restroom is for customers only."

"I'm not going there. I'd like to order a white wine on the patio."

"I'll be right with you."

"Take your time. There's no rush." I take off my ADOPT A DOG sign and stuff it in my purse. I fix my hair and wipe my perspiring face with a tissue. I walk out to the patio and stop at their table.

"How refreshing your white wine looks. May I ask which one you got?" I ask the blonde.

"It's a Chardonnay from some region in Italy," she replies without looking at me.

"Perfect, that's what I'll order. I couldn't help but overhear a bit of your conversation. I'm looking to buy a dog. Where is your shop located?"

"We have a terrific selection. It's down two blocks on the corner of First," the blonde says, more friendly now. She smiles with a full set of capped teeth and glances at my dress. Her eyes are cold blue. The redhead doesn't say anything.

"Wonderful. Good day, ladies. Excuse me, I need to go to the restroom."

I walk back into the restaurant and slip into the restroom before exiting through the front door. Luckily, the waitress never sees me because she's too busy serving customers.

The dogs sit up to kiss me as I squat to pet and untie them. We walk around the corner so my prospective employers don't see me. I take out my sign and put it back on, and then open the dog food container and pour the kibble directly on the cement into two piles. Mr. Bull and Athenia gobble it up until there is not a shred left. Tomorrow I will go to the pet shop and get my part-time sales job.

We head all the way back up to Central Park, and by the time we get there, about an hour later, we are very thirsty. We quench our thirst at a water fountain, and decide to take a rest near the tennis courts, under a large, old, familiar tree. I lean against its soft bark and sink slowly to the ground while the back-and-forth sound of the tennis balls lulls me into thoughts about the job at the pet shop.

It would be such a relief to get it. One less thing to worry about. Interviews are painful. The prospective employer asks too many personal questions, and when you tell the truth, he or she thinks something is wrong with you. Employers try to hide their feelings, but facial expressions rarely lie. "Why were you let go?" they ask. Nobody believes it was because of a merger; good employees aren't let go. Then they want to know why you haven't worked at other marketing jobs. And though they'll never admit it, they don't like that you are on the wrong side of sixty. I've never wanted to work for a pet shop, because I don't believe animals should be commodities. There are too many unwanted ones who should be the first to be placed in homes. But I'll make an exception this time. Both women seem professional, and who knows, maybe they'll want to adopt a few of the shelter dogs.

The breeze caresses my face and the dogs lick my fingers. Comforted, I fall asleep. When I awake, it's dark. I don't know what time it is, but there are few people in the park, so by New York standards it is very late.

"Why didn't you wake me?" I anxiously ask the dogs. I stand and tug on their leashes. Mr. Bull stands to attention, ready to march. Athenia wants to be picked up, so I carry her. If Mr. Bull could carry both of us, I'm sure he would.

The front door to the animal center is closed and locked. Why don't I seem able to follow Sheila's rules anymore? I have always been obedient. I have always tried to be on the best side of management. I think these adoption walks are eating at me. They start off filled with hope and then end with a sense of futility. The contrast is becoming intolerable.

We have no place to sleep and I would like to shower. I hold Athenia and Mr. Bull tightly and give them each a kiss. We sit down at the entrance to the shelter's driveway and stare at the white half-moon.

"I have no desire to ride a spaceship to the moon. I like looking at it from a distance," I say.

The dogs respond by cuddling closer against my legs.

It is quiet. I hear crickets. In the moonlight I see weeds sprouting up from the small cracks of cement. Life has a way of asserting itself, even in the most modest conditions. A little bit of soil, water, and sun is all it takes. And what crack do I grow from?

The dogs howl. A young policeman in a patrol car stops. He gets out. He has soft eyes. Mr. Bull barks and Athenia hides behind my back.

"Lady, are you hurt?"

"You don't have to bother with me."

"You're sitting in an active driveway. You could get run over."

"They're closed."

"Why are you sitting there?"

I point to the animal center. "I'm waiting for them to open."

"Morning is a long way off. You can't sit here 'til then."

"I have nothing more important to do."

"Can I see some ID?"

"Left it in my house."

"Where is that?"

"Oh, downtown."

"Are these your dogs?"

"Yes."

"I'm going to leave now. When I come back in five minutes you'd better be gone. Do you understand?"

"Yes. Say good-bye to the kind officer." Mr. Bull and Athenia bark.

I know a kind officer when I meet one. This is not the first time I've been stopped for sitting around at night. When the marshals sealed my apartment door, I was in shock for days. The police felt sorry for me when I pretended I needed to get back into my apartment to retrieve my dog. When they broke the lock, they realized I didn't have a dog but allowed me to pack a bag anyway.

We walk to a nearby brownstone and sit on the top stair. The same police officer drives by and stops. He rolls down his window.

"You don't hear very well."

"I moved."

"Please, ma'am, you know there is no loitering in public places. Go to a shelter if you have to, but most don't take dogs."

"You're right, it's late. We'll head home. I will not trouble you again."

"Very well then."

He watches us stand and start to walk from his forbidden zone, then drives off. We walk to the park, where I know a secret hiding place. Once we get into the park, we tuck ourselves behind the pink rose bushes. I don't feel like such a freak sleeping here with my friends. I don't have to make up excuses or lie about my circumstances. I can let my guard down, even cry. Athenia and Mr. Bull will still love me.

The roses are lovely. "I won't pick you until I have a vase to put you in," I tell them. I envision my old mahogany end table and my blue-and-white vase overflowing with flowers. I loved filling that vase weekly with all different types of flowers. My ex-husband had allergies and blamed me for them, so I stopped buying flowers and kept the vase empty —until he cheated on me. Then I bought fresh-cut pink roses every four days and placed them in the vase next to my alarm clock on my bedside table. He coughed and sneezed and eventually moved into the living room. That was the beginning of the end. Communication and respect broke down and neither one of us cared much about what we did or said to the other.

Mr. Bull snores just like an old congested man. Athenia snuggles under my arm like a sweet baby girl and barely makes a sound when she sleeps. Their bodies are warm and comforting. Yes, I'd rather be homeless than live in a place that doesn't allow pets.

● ● ●

The morning sun beats on my face. We are well rested and prepared to face the sunny ninety-degree day. We arrive at the animal center during rush hour. Sheila is standing rigidly with her hands in her pockets, glaring at us.

"I screwed up! I'm so sorry," I hasten to say, not wanting to hear her lecture again.

"You look like a wreck." Sheila shakes her head, eyeing my clothes and my sneakers, which are coming dangerously loose at the seams.

"I'll adopt her. I'll even adopt him. I hate to think of what might happen to them, or me, if I don't. Please trust me again."

"Now tell me, how do you intend to adopt them?" Sheila says as she begins to unwrap a new computer. I take in its sleek, new contours. "It just came in," she explains.

"I'm looking for a place to live that allows pets."

"I'll need an address. You know, an official place of residence. Now do you have an address that I can put down on the application?"

"Like I said, I'm looking for a new place."

"I know that, but the form doesn't know that."

"Give them your address."

"For how long?"

"I don't know."

She mulls this over for a moment as she removes more plastic wrapping from the computer. "I hate to lie, but I will this time because it's for you. I'll need your new address by next week."

"Yes, you'll have it."

"Promise?"

I meet her questioning eyes and nod with conviction.

"Oh, also, take these new adoption forms. I forgot to give them to you."

"Every month they create a new form," I observe, taking the forms and a pen from her and stuffing them into my overloaded purse. They barely fit. "Thanks."

Sheila walks back to her desk and efficiently opens the mail. Her routine is robotic. She sifts through mostly direct mail solicitations, setting aside the few important items into a save pile and tossing the rest directly into the garbage can stationed between her legs.

"See you later," Sheila says, then looks up at me. "Right?"

"Yes, dear."

A volunteer hurries up to me and greets me courteously. "Good morning, Miss Pink. I just thought you might want to know that a beaten black lab came in last night."

Sheila says to me, "You can leave the dogs up here with me."

"What happened?" I ask the volunteer.

"Take a look and see what you think."

I ask Sheila if it's okay, and she responds, "Didn't I just say you can leave those two with me? I don't say what I don't mean, you should know that by now."

As I turn to walk away, Athenia and Mr. Bull whimper in protest. "Not to worry, dears, I'll be back." I hug them and they believe me.

As I open the back door to the kennels, the stench of

desperation almost makes me pass out. I steady myself and keep walking with the help of the Serenity Prayer, which my ex-husband learned in AA and passed along to me: *God grant me the serenity to accept the things I cannot change, the courage to change the things I can, and the wisdom to know the difference.* Whenever I feel overwhelmed, these words can help to calm me down and allow me to think clearly.

The animals are beside themselves with grief and anxiety. For now I'm their only hope. I'm headed to the second row at the end. Through the bars I can see the burned back of a large black dog. Cigarette burns cover almost every square inch of his bleeding, puss-infected back. As calm as I try to remain, the sight of this injustice fills me with righteous rage. I imagine taking a blowtorch to the bare back of the dog's abuser. Such sweet revenge!

The overzealous volunteer is standing next to the black lab's cage. She looks at me dryly. "He's violent. Bit the last volunteer when she tried to feed him."

"You would too if you were treated like that."

"I'm here to tell you to be careful."

"I'll be no less careful than I would be with you."

"Look, I don't know what your issue is with me. Why are you always jumping down my throat?"

"It's not personal," I state.

"Yes, I think it is."

"My time is limited, and I can't get into a discussion about the causes and effects of abuse," I say as calmly as I can. Creating a problem for Sheila is not a smart strategy, so I simply add, "Have a nice day."

She hands me a large milk bone and a thick glove. "You'll

need this."

"Thank you," I say, taking the bone and ignoring the glove. She stands there sullenly.

I open the cage and sit patiently in front of it, waving the bone in the black lab's line of vision.

"I wouldn't do that if I were you."

"You aren't me."

"Aren't you afraid?"

I laugh. "Of what?"

"Of getting hurt."

"I used to be. Come here, Blacky." I take a bite of the bone. "Not bad."

"You are gross," the volunteer says.

I take another bite. I wave it again in front of Blacky. "Try it. You'll like it."

"Disgusting."

Blacky observes my every move. I lie on my back on the floor and call out gently, "Oh Blacky, please come out and play."

He comes out of his cage and smells my face. I pet him as he nuzzles my side and whimpers. The overzealous volunteer has left to go clean cages, so I say to no one in particular, "Forgive them, for they know not what they do." I put a leash on the lab and we walk into the reception area to join Mr. Bull and Athenia.

Sheila loosely holds their leashes and when they see me she lets them fall to the floor. They run up and jump on me. Then they turn to Blacky and smell him. Athenia licks his paw and Mr. Bull licks his ear. The newcomer sits down and lets Athenia gently lick his largest open sore. Blacky wags his tail in gratitude. The show of empathy and kindness and trust is deeply moving.

"If only the human race could do this," Sheila says, her eyes welling with tears.

Athenia leans on me, wanting to be picked up. "The animals have a lot to teach us," I agree, embracing Athenia.

Sheila stuffs three cans of dog food in a bag and hands it to me along with fifty dollars.

"Thank you very much, but what's the money for?"

"Take it and buy yourself new sneakers."

"I can't."

"You must."

"How will I pay you back?"

"You already do, daily."

I lower my head in appreciation. "Thank you for the money that I so need."

"Good luck today," she says.

We parade out in single file, and when I look back, Sheila is smiling. It's always reassuring to see your boss smile behind your back.

When we get to Union Square, which is a few miles away, there is a makeshift 9-11 memorial. Why today, I haven't a clue. It's still August. There are photos of the dead with personal text underneath describing their deeds on earth and how much they were loved. It's moving, and I wonder if similar photos and descriptions of shelter dogs might be an effective tool for animal adoption. I walk around a circle of born-again Christians singing together, Jehovah's witnesses handing out literature, rappers dancing, and journalists interviewing the many bystanders. A middle-aged, black-haired, blue-eyed man with a crooked smile approaches me. He's wearing a sign that says JEWS FOR JESUS. I'm hoping he'll want to adopt one of the dogs, so I smile at him.

"All you have to do is say you're a sinner and Jesus will take you into heaven after you die," he informs me.

"And what about them?" I ask, indicating the dogs.

"They can't go to heaven unless they are baptized," he replies.

"Is it possible they can find heaven on earth?"

"The Bible says—"

"Now, now," I interject, "don't use others' words. Use your own."

"If you don't believe in the Bible, you are a sinner."

"Dogs don't need a Bible to live the truth," I say, with no intention of waiting for a response. As I turn to walk away, the sneaker on my left foot rips apart, so I remove both sneakers and proceed barefoot toward a garbage can.

"Don't walk away from the truth!" he yells after me.

I realize he's following me now, so I stop and dangle my sneakers in his face.

"What else does one do with items that are no longer useful?" Then I throw both sneakers into the garbage. A short man wearing a dirty sweat suit takes them out and puts them on his feet. But they are in such bad shape, he takes them off and throws them back in.

A preacher in a clerical collar yells out to the milling crowd: "Don't forget to read your Bible!"

"Are you guys hiring part-time office help?" I ask him.

"No, we don't hire. We recruit."

"I suppose that means you don't pay."

"That's right."

A group of Hare Krishnas passes us, playing their string instruments and banging on small colorful drums, singing, "Hare Krishna Hare Krishna, Krishna Krishna Hare Hare, Hare Rama Hare Rama, Rama Rama Hare Hare . . ."

I whisper to my dogs, "We humans are so consumed with this belief and that belief and 'my belief is the only belief' and 'I am right' and 'you are wrong' and on and on until we all become simply stupid. You dogs are more fortunate in a way because you don't have to defend your identity."

My feet are bleeding now. The time has come to buy a new pair of sneakers. There are many stores surrounding the square, so it should not be too difficult. On the other hand, I am particular about shoes. These days I prefer classic light-colored sneakers that are compatible with the several pink outfits I lost weight to fit into.

I used to shop at high-end department stores and buy matching shoes for my many outfits. I also wore padded bras so that my nipples wouldn't protrude through my silk blouses. Everything I wore was in classically good taste. Nothing flashy, nothing low cut, and nothing that would make anyone look twice. During my magazine days, I liked dark colors that would help me blend into the background and keep my clients' needs up front.

I find a storefront window exhibiting mostly high heels, but there are a few trendy ballet slipper designs and attractive sneakers. I motion to the long-haired sales lady, asking her if I can bring my pooches in. She hesitates briefly, then nods yes.

"Just in time," she says, noticing my bare feet.

"It's not as bad as it looks. At least it's warm out. Any sneakers in pink?"

"You are in the right place. What size?"

"Seven."

She notices Blacky's damaged back and says, "Holy shit, what happened?"

"He needs a new home so this won't happen again. Would you like to bring him home?"

"Home? What's that?" She laughs.

"I've often asked myself the same question." I laugh too.

"I'm just never home. Between school and work, I only sleep there."

"He's a good companion, very sweet."

Smiling, she says, "Would you please wash your feet before you try the shoes on?"

"Of course, dear."

"The bathroom is down the hall," she says, pointing toward the back. I take my dogs and we go into a clean bathroom that's just big enough to fit all four of us. I wash the blood off my feet and pour water into the dogs' plastic container. I wipe down the sink and the black-and-white tiled floor and return to the nice sales lady. No other customers are in the store.

"Here, try these. They are the last pair of this style." She hands me the most beautiful pair of pink sneakers. They slip on easily, in the same way a pair of satin Christian Dior shoes would.

"Now I can walk on anything." I strut up and down the aisle, looking in all the mirrors. The heel of one sneaker slips off a few times, so I tighten the laces.

"How do they feel?"

"Perfect," I say.

"They look great, but they're too big."

"I'll grow into them."

"Stuff the toes with tissue. It will help."

"Good idea. That's exactly what I'll do."

"So you are going to take them?"

"Yes. How much?"

"Forty-one dollars plus tax."

"Perfect." I give her the precious fifty-dollar bill Sheila gave to me and thank her. Then I ask in my most professional tone if she needs any sales help. She shakes her head and flatly says no. "But thank you for your business," she graciously adds before leaving to service another customer. This reminds me of how I used to feel every time I made a sale: as if the client had saved my life. At those moments, I would float on the sense of accomplishment, confident that I was valuable and needed.

Wearing my new shoes, we head downtown to the East Village where the redheaded woman's pet shop is. When I turn the corner on First Avenue, tucked in between a deli and a stationery store is a yellow-painted awning with the words: PUPPIES FOR SALE. I stop to look through the storefront window and find two furry little puppies jumping about playfully. One is rolling a small red rubber ball while the other is trying to challenge him to a duel. Standing behind the counter is the blonde pet store manager. There is a sign on the door: NO PETS ALLOWED BUT THE ONES YOU BUY. I walk down the block, a few buildings away, and tie my dogs to a leafy tree.

"Stay. I'll be back."

They wag their tails, but Blacky barks anxiously. He looks at me with those penetrating, light-grey eyes. He resembles a wolf, half wise and half wild with the knowledge of abuse and abandonment. I pet him until he calms down.

Then I wrap my dirty hair in a bun, put on my pink baseball hat, and walk up to the pet shop. When I enter, the blonde looks at me as if she's never seen me before.

Smiling, she says, "Can I help you?"

Relieved that she doesn't recognize me from the café, I take in the layout of the store and reply, "Not yet, dear. I'll look around and let you know."

"Okay."

I walk around pretending to be interested in the pet supplies. I hear the blonde manager talking harshly to a disgruntled employee. "As I was saying, make sure the bottom of the cages are cleaned tonight." She grabs a soiled newspaper from one of the cages and throws it in the garbage. The puppy retreats to the corner. "How many times do I have to tell you the same thing?"

"Sorry," the young employee responds.

The manager picks up a rubber ball and puts it under the employee's nose.

"Dust the rubber toys, too."

"Yes."

"I don't know how many months you've been living in the city, but you still move like you are from the corn fields."

"I'm from Scarsdale."

"Outside of Manhattan it's all a farm."

The employee lowers her head.

The manager announces loudly to anyone within earshot: "I need to have an employee who moves like a hungry tiger. 'Eat them alive' is my motto."

The employee says softly, "I'm sorry, I'm just not feeling good these days."

"My store doesn't have to suffer for that." She opens the cash register, takes out a hundred-dollar bill, and stuffs it into her black pants pocket.

The employee plays with a baby bulldog in a cage.

"Stop playing with him. The customers do that."

"I can't help it."

The manager rolls her eyes and approaches me. "Are you sure you don't need assistance?" Her tone is one of great annoyance.

"No, thank you, dear."

I decide to leave now because there is poison in the air and I don't want to inhale any more of it. When I get back to the dogs, they are lying flat on the cement beneath the tree, waiting patiently. When I see them there, I realize that I'm a hungry tiger and I need that sales job now, so I go back to the shop. When I open the door, it is quiet with the exceptions of a few weak barks.

The manager smiles. "You're back. Welcome. So you want to know how much that puppy is in the window?"

"Perhaps."

"You know, a purebred is a good investment."

"The baby bulldog is cute."

The employee must be hiding in the back because I don't see her.

"I'll give you a good price."

"The girl who was just here before, where is she?"

"She left from the back exit. Why? You know her?"

The cages are filthy. "No, it's just that these cages need cleaning. I'm a good cleaner and I could help out."

"You looking for a job?"

"Yes, part time."

"Won't do, I need full time."

"Okay, I'll take it."

"Hold on a moment, nobody is hiring you so fast. What are your abilities?"

"I can groom, sell, mop."

"Sell?"

"That was my profession. I can sell anything. I was so good, I memorized every area code in the country."

"I certainly do need a multitasker. Someone who knows how to answer phones, who's pleasant with customers, up to speed on inventory, an expert at cleaning cages, grooming, floor sweeping—sort of like a Wall Street commodities trader, if you know what I mean. Do you sincerely feel you can achieve this?"

"Yes."

"References, I'll need some."

"Sheila at Animal Care Center, and Dr. Pauly on Central Park. Oh, but he's out of town."

"Don't tell me, show me."

"Yes, I understand."

"What is your name?"

"Miss Pink. And yours?"

"Sally."

"Nice name."

"I don't pay above minimum wage."

"Can I start now?"

"Tomorrow morning, at nine o'clock sharp. If you are late, I'll dock your pay fifty cents for each ten-minute interval. Do you understand?"

"Very well."

"Thank goodness you have a low sense of entitlement, not like the last one."

"What do you mean?"

"Impossible girl. Whatever I said she challenged."

"Not me."

"That's because you've been in the work force and at your age if you haven't learned the rules of the game then you're good for nothing. I'm sure you know by now there are many in line waiting to do what you do. We are all disposable. It's survival of the fittest."

"I look forward to a long, fruitful relationship," I tell her, hoping I can keep this job long enough to get a place to live and adopt as many dogs as possible.

"Just do your job." She opens the door.

"Thank you very much. You won't be disappointed. Bless you," I say and exit the shop.

Sally shuts the door behind me and I skip like a schoolgirl down the street to the dogs. Passersby stare at me for a moment, but in New York we each do our thing without paying much attention to others. Unless you are a half-naked, twenty-two-year-old supermodel in yellow patent-leather high heels, you can pretty much do whatever you like without attracting attention.

● ● ●

When I arrive back at the shelter, Sheila is not there. A new volunteer is answering the phones. I introduce myself and ask her where Sheila is. She tells me something happened to Sheila's aunt and she has gone to attend to her. I share with this volunteer what Sheila and I have agreed to. It doesn't seem to affect her one way or another. Her tattoos are dramatic images of Native American royalty. I doubt she knows which chiefs adorn her shoulder and arm. They resemble Edward Curtis photographs depicting a proud culture. Her upper arm is too thin for the feathered crown, so the feathers are lost in her armpit.

"I'm going back there," I say, pointing to the kennel.

"Okay."

I take all three dogs to the kennel area. They bark and whimper and try to run back out toward the reception area. I pull them back into the kennel.

"Don't worry, dears. Mommy will be back soon." I intend to give myself a few hours to find a place to live.

First, I look for a cage for Blacky. He'd prefer to be alone, but there are no empty cages. I attempt to put him in with a depressed mutt, half pug and half hound, but I quickly remove Blacky to search for a more compatible cage mate. Finally, three cages later, he's agreed to share a cage with an old sheltie. The sheltie looks exactly like the one from the park the other day. I remember the distinct marking on the sheltie's right paw because it resembles a Rorschach inkblot. I'm furious.

"How dare she give you away," I say to the sheltie. "I'm going to find your owner and give her a piece of my mind. Then I'm going to get back my stolen money from her husband. Then I'm going to find a loving home for you." I see the sheltie's name tag has been removed.

Another new volunteer appears. I anxiously ask her, "Do we have an address for the sheltie?"

"Sheila knows."

"When is she coming back?"

"I don't know."

"What *do* you know?' I ask irritably.

"I don't work for you," she says.

"You are new here and I want to let you in on a fact. And that is, here we all work together and toward one goal, which is to help the animals. So check the ego at the door."

I lock Blacky's cage shut. He's aggravated and bites at the bars, then takes a nip at the sheltie. I take out the sheltie and put her in another cage. She seems mild-mannered, so I think she might get along with Brownie. But when I put her in with Brownie, he growls and nips. Each time I go to pick her up again, she wags her tail. She is used to affection. She has been loved and therefore she can love. Athenia shakes and won't leave me. I pry her away and stick her in with three puppies and the sheltie. She quiets down and the sheltie licks her.

But then the vet appears with a grim expression on his face. I decide it would be safest to take them all out of the cages and go to the park until Shelia returns. The sheltie is grateful for this turn of events. When I take her back out of the cage, she rolls on her back and lies there with her legs in the air until I pet her. Then she affectionately pats my forearm with her front paw. I must find her owner.

I lead Athenia, Mr. Bull, Blacky, and the sheltie to the park, where we will spend the night. Along the way, the other dogs smell the sheltie and lick her, and she does the same until their leashes get tangled. I've rarely seen a dog enjoy other dogs as much as this sheltie does. Until now, she must have been isolated from other dogs and desperate to make contact with her four-legged brothers and sisters. But she is old, so we have to stop often to let her sit and rest.

CHAPTER EIGHT

If I let the sheltie show me her routine, I'll find her mother. She guides us through the park to all her pee spots. She pulls on her leash so hard that I think her neck will break. We follow her out of the park and down the street to a doorman building on West 63rd Street and Central Park West. The surprised doorman comes out and pets the sheltie.

"Abigail, your mother has been worried sick about you. Where were you?"

"Hello, sir. Where is her mother?"

"Upstairs."

"I'd like to talk with her."

"And you are?"

"Miss Pink."

"Why do you have Abigail?"

"I found her."

"Mrs. Wolf needs this dog. Poor woman, they're torturing her."

Apparently she changed her name, but I know who she is and she can't outsmart me.

"May I speak with her?"

Clean-shaven men wearing navy-blue FBI sweatshirts walk

out of the building carrying boxes and envelopes. One bends down to pet Blacky on the forehead. Blacky wiggles his tail. The doorman opens the door for the men and they load everything into a black SUV.

"And your name, please?"

"Miss Pink."

"Oh yes, you told me already. My apologies." He dials and announces my name. He tells her that I have Abigail with me and is promptly ordered to send me up.

He escorts me into the marble-and-bronze elevator. He presses the PH2 button and turns to the dog. "Welcome home, Abigail."

The door closes and all the dogs sit quietly. The elevator door opens and standing there waiting for us is the blonde woman I saw in the park. Abigail wags her tail and Mrs. Wolf cries out in relief. The woman has a large bandage on her head.

"They attacked me and left me for dead." She strokes her bandaged head to indicate where they knocked her.

"You deserve it, after what you did."

"Who are you?"

"I'm the one who saved your dog, that's who I am."

"Thank God."

"You should be ashamed of giving her away."

"Give her away? What are you talking about? They kidnapped her."

"Who?"

"I never saw them before. They looked pretty normal until they attacked me."

"They must have had a reason."

"They accused me of helping my husband steal money."
She hugs the sheltie and says, "Abby, you look thin. Those
bastards."

"She was left at the animal control center, which is not a
Canyon Ranch resort. They have a kill policy."

"She is my baby. I raised her."

"It does not give you the right to throw her away because
you're desperate."

"I did no such thing. How dare you stand there and
accuse me of such treatment! Are you with the press?"

"No."

"Then don't act like a moron."

"Listen, Madoff, I know who you are. You owe me big
time. I saved your dog. So this is what I want. First, I want
my money back from your husband, and then I want you to
adopt these dogs."

She smiles wearily and says, "I'm not Madoff. People
mistake me for Ruth because I resemble her."

"You aren't his wife?"

"I met her once at a fundraiser. I'm sorry, I can't help
you."

"Yes, you can. Adopt them." Mr. Bull, Athenia, and
Blacky are all huddled close against my legs.

"It doesn't look like these dogs want to leave you."

"Maybe not, but there are many others."

"I don't have a place to live anymore."

"What about here?"

"The government seized it and will be selling it along
with everything else I own."

"What did you do?"

"My husband was unfairly convicted of doing what Bernie did. Just because they met a couple of times, he's being used as a scapegoat."

"How could a mistake like this happen?"

"How could any injustice happen? It happened! I'm telling you, they convicted an innocent man."

"And I thought I had problems," I say, relenting a little.

"This is like the French Revolution. They'd take my head if they could. They took away my home in Florida, and South Hampton. They even took my cappuccino machine. But I can offer you a tea."

"I'm not sure I should come in. My shoes are dirty."

"Take them off."

"My feet aren't clean."

"I haven't gotten a pedicure in weeks. I couldn't care less what your toes look like."

"Thank you, but I don't want to come in." The thought of this beautiful home overlooking the park being taken away from her is painful.

"How about cookies for the dogs?"

"Ask them."

"Cookie? Cookie?" she offers in an inviting, high-pitched tone. They bark excitedly in response. She waves them all in. They follow her, and so do I.

"Okay, we'll stay for a minute," I say.

Abigail proudly escorts us down a long, wide corridor. Mrs. Wolf walks behind her dog and we follow. The marble foyer is filled with large wooden crates and there is not a stick of furniture left in the massive living room, which resembles an eighteenth-century Italian ballroom with a fresco painted on the ceiling. Mrs. Wolf shows me around the empty five-bedroom apartment. There are no lighting fixtures. All the bulbs are bare. The only furniture left is a king-sized Posturepedic mattress on the white-carpeted floor in her master bedroom.

"There must have been beautiful paintings hanging on those walls."

"Yes. I was an art collector."

"Where is everything?"

"Gone. The Feds took it to pay the investors back."

"If he's innocent, this is a great injustice."

"What's worse, I had to spend all our money to defend him. What a system! I ask you, who is the gonif?"

"Gonif?"

"Yes, that's Yiddish for thief."

"Where will you go?"

"To my sister-in-law's house on Long Island. She says she lost money with her brother. She'll torture me with her whining."

"How unfortunate."

"Thank God it's temporary. Listen," she whispers, "if you do something for me, I'll do something for you."

"Nobody is here."

"The walls have ears."

"I did something for you already. Now you owe me," I remind her.

"What do you want?" she asks.

"Homes for many dogs, like I said."

"And for yourself?" she asks.

"The truth," I tell her.

"You mean the big-picture truth, like why do we exist? Or more personal, like why do you exist?"

"Your truth."

"I don't know why I exist," Mrs. Wolf says.

"I mean whether or not your husband stole from all those innocent people. Swear on Abigail's life to tell me the truth."

"Let's put it this way: I always understood that my husband was a brilliant financial mind, and if the market hadn't turned, nobody would have been hurt."

"So the market is to blame?"

"Market, schmarket, everyone is to blame. But good can come from this. I can help you with the dogs, but in my own way, and you must keep your mouth shut and do something for me."

"I have nothing to give you."

She tiptoes into her bedroom and indicates for me to follow her. The sheltie remains outside in the hallway, but my dogs follow me. She puts her hand up and says in her normal voice: "No animals allowed on my white carpet."

"Stay," I command.

"I opened my big mouth," she whispers. "Now the Feds know which room we're in. What can I do, they are making me meshuga. You understand?"

"Yeah, I know a little Yiddish."

I follow her into her bathroom.

She suddenly announces in a loud voice, "I have the best exercise tape. It will make you lose ten pounds!"

"I beg your pardon, are you calling me fat?"

She whispers in my ear, "Oy vey, were you born yesterday? The apartment is *bugged*."

She turns on an old boom box. Then she opens the vanity's top drawer, takes out a tile cutter, and cuts into a loose tile on the shower wall. It cracks in half and behind it is a black plastic bag. She unties it. Inside is a purple velvet satchel, which she also unties.

"Marilyn Monroe had to schtup many men to get what I have here. I only had to marry one."

Glittering under the bare bulbs are many diamond rings and necklaces. She takes out a necklace and puts the bag back behind the cracked tile. She turns off the boom box and loudly announces, "In six days they expect me out of here. I'm almost packed. I'll be ready."

We walk out of her bedroom. Abigail jumps up for affection. Mrs. Wolf pets her several times, then takes her necklace and strings it comfortably around Athenia's neck.

"What a beautiful little princess this one is," she says about the newly adorned Athenia, then says to Abby, "Say thank you to your fairy godmother." Mrs. Wolf turns to me. "She says thank you. It's so nice of you to walk Abby." She knows the FBI is listening. "My legs are getting worse. But if I'm feeling better, I'll meet you at Strawberry Fields tomorrow. Come and get Abigail at ten. She'll be ready." Mrs. Wolf winks.

"I can't at ten. How about six in the evening?"

"Fine, that will do."

"We've got to go," I tell her. We head back down the elevator as Feds are entering the lobby. One bends down to casually pet Athenia's head. I inwardly gasp. Could he have overheard anything?

We are back on the crowded streets in the intense heat. A

far cry from Mrs. Wolf's temperature-controlled apartment. Everywhere I turn there are cop cars and ambulance sirens. Something is happening. Now come the fire truck sirens. There must be a fire, maybe in the Time Warner building. They are heading that way. The roads are blocked by double-parked cars. The honking is deafening. I keep turning back to see if I'm being tailed by the FBI. *Keep walking*, I tell myself, *don't let anyone get in your way*. Crowds are everywhere. I weave around groups of people and some try to pet the dogs. Normally I would allow it, but now I'm anxious to keep moving. I zigzag through the park in an attempt to lose my imaginary pursuers. Fortunately, I know every square inch of this park.

It's getting dark and I need to secure a place for all of us to sleep. Tomorrow is my big day, and I'm excited for the job to start. I'll need a good night's sleep, but I'm also hungry and tired, and so are the dogs. I search through garbage to find only a few gnawed barbecued ribs for the dogs, nothing edible for myself. So I find a water fountain and tell myself that tonight I'm on a liquid diet, cleansing my liver and kidneys. Choosing to give my digestive system a break helps to make the hunger go away. I tuck us behind a cluster of bushes and hang my shirt on a tree so it doesn't wrinkle. I'm glad to see that my bodysuit underneath has protected the shirt from underarm stains. The air is stifling, no hint of a breeze. Nonetheless, with my devoted companions nestled near me, I sleep like a baby.

At daybreak I arrive at the animal center to see Sheila pacing back and forth. Seeing her is almost always a relief. She's highly capable and has answers to all kinds of problems. When she sees us, she smiles.

I show her my new shoes and then I announce, "Finding homes is getting more difficult in this economy. We'll have to build a no-kill shelter."

"What happened to 'Hello, how are you? How's your aunt?'"

"I'm sorry. How is your aunt?"

"Having a nervous breakdown."

"I'm so sorry."

"They are giving her heavy meds. And it's all because of Madoff, the prick."

"I hope she feels better soon," I offer.

"She will when she accepts her loss. She's still fighting it. She's a wreck."

"She's lucky to have you," I say. I hand her the change left over from purchasing the sneakers. "And so am I. Thanks. I'll never forget your kindness. It came at a perfect time because I just got a job at a pet shop. The only problem is I can't bring in the dogs."

"Keep the change, Miss Pink. But you're not allowed to leave your adopted pets here. Our resources are maxed out."

"They are not officially adopted. I didn't complete all the paperwork."

"Not a good argument."

"Jesus, Sheila, I'm stuck. Help us out." I realize she's already been helping us out and I'm pushing my luck, but what else can I do?

"Only a few days, that's it. I'll write 'pending adoption' on the form."

"They hate cages."

"You know they can't stay up here with me."

By now Blacky has become very attached to me and won't even go near Sheila when she calls for him so she can inspect his wounds.

"He's a problem," Sheila says.

"Why?"

"He's gotten too close to you."

"Is that considered antisocial behavior?"

"Potentially. It could prevent him from getting adopted."

"He's damned if he gets too close, and damned if he doesn't. It's a rigged situation."

The overzealous volunteer runs up to us and, gesturing to my crew, asks Sheila, "Should we feed them?"

Sheila looks at me, then replies, "For today."

"They will appreciate it," I say.

Time is running tight. I have enough change for a one-way subway trip down to the pet shop. Thank God Sheila let me keep the change.

● ● ●

When I arrive at the pet shop, it's exactly 9:00 a.m. Sally points to her watch as I enter.

"You cut it close. If it were my first day, I'd come ten minutes earlier."

"Yes."

"Here, take this cloth. Wipe down those shelves, clean the smelly piss from those cages, and answer the phone.

"Yes."

I do it all thoroughly and efficiently, and I do it with style.

I even have time left over to play with the puppies.

"Do not play with them."

"I can do both."

"That's what the other one said, and I fired her. Mop over there. I see mouse droppings."

"The food attracts them."

"Obviously. And it's not my problem now, it's yours."

"I love solving problems."

"You have plenty of them here."

"God never gives us more than we can handle. Unless he hates us."

"Don't give me clichés. I have no use for them. It's all a matter of will. If you can't use it to get things done, you are no use to society. Have you ever heard of Ayn Rand?"

"No." I will not tell her I read *The Fountainhead* and *Atlas Shrugged* like most educated women of my generation. I will not tell her I thought they were one-dimensional and lacked spiritual love.

"Do yourself a favor and read *Atlas Shrugged*. Ms. Rand was a genius. Even Alan Greenspan is a loyal follower. You think he doesn't know anything?"

"I don't know what he knows."

"He's a powerful man."

"Yes."

"He's a pure capitalist. He knows how to use man's will to achieve."

"Man's will or man's needs?"

"Read *Atlas Shrugged*. You'll learn."

Apparently, being condescending is part of Sally's management technique. Not responding is part of mine. I politely excuse myself and go about emptying cage debris into black plastic bags and petting puppies. But she follows me, arguing on and on about female dominance in the business world. Foam is now forming at the corners of her red lipsticked mouth: "Without economic freedom, we would be chattel, nothing more than men's property. Women can now use money for power just like men. We can buy ourselves into politics and corporate boards and cause great changes in policies around the globe. But most women still don't get it. They still think sex is the way to freedom. A man will fall on his knees for a dollar, not pussy. Because pussy is abundant. Money is not."

I must have missed those pages in *The Fountainhead*. When she's finished giving me her crass lesson on business, she orders, "Go to the storeroom and unload the three boxes from the corner."

"I'm not finished cleaning all the cages."

"They can wait."

"But the paper is wet and the little ones will be uncomfortable."

"What's more important?"

"The puppies."

"Wrong!"

"They'll get sick."

"They are actually less profitable than the rest of our inventory. I have a better markup on collars, toys, dishes and leashes. The leashes are a gold mine."

She follows me into the storage area. I feel her scrutinizing me with those cold, sociopathic eyes as I carefully unpack each item, dusting the small plastic packing pellets off the new merchandise and stacking it carefully on the metal shelves. Then she follows me out.

"The other one was so clumsy. She dropped three water dishes when I asked her a question."

"Some people are nervous," I say.

Sally leans on the sales counter. "Always crying. She couldn't see through the tears."

I hang the leashes on the racks. "I like the petal pink and baby blue leashes," I say. "I think a lot of people will."

Sally reaches into the last box, as if searching for something. "Shit, they never arrived." She picks up the phone and dials. "Hello. Bob, the boxes with the leashes never arrived."

"Yes, they are here," I whisper.

She doesn't look at me and continues to bark at Bob on the phone. "I said they didn't arrive. Now that you screwed up my order, send another shipment and don't you dare charge me for it. You owe me."

"They're here." I hold up the pink and blue leashes to show her.

"Tomorrow then." She slams the phone down.

"Sally, there is a misunderstanding. Here they are."

"You don't know how to run a company. This is called leveraging. I'm not asking for your input."

"I thought you'd want to know . . ."

"You are not paid to think."

"It just happens. I can't help it."

"Don't answer back. Just do your job," she snaps.

I can't believe the nerve of this woman, but I can't afford to lose this job, so I bite my tongue and take the new neon-blue leashes back and hang them on the racks. Then I stack the water dishes and organize packages of pet food according to brand. Organic goes on one side, and all the rest goes on the other. I stack the more philanthropic dog food brands in front of the others. For example, I have read that Halo donates to small, lesser-known shelters that are hard up for funding, so I give those bags more prominent placement.

The day passes quickly. Only a few customers enter, which is good because I can learn the merchandise layout, the pricing, and, most important, Sally's rigid ways. By the time the day is over, every cage is clean and every puppy has been spoken to, kissed, and hugged. Sally leaves earlier than I do, but only after spending an hour teaching me how to lock up. It is a simple process, but she asks me to rehearse it ten times. Lock, unlock, put on the alarm, turn off the alarm, leave one light on, lower the air conditioning, turn voice mail on, turn voice mail off—all repeated to the point of disorientation.

● ● ●

The neon-orange sun sets behind the Hudson River, now half in the water and half in the psychedelic sky. I have to find a place to rent before I go back to the shelter. I don't want to keep the dogs in cages or sleep in the park for another day. I go to the Bowery, where I know there are several rooming houses. Hopefully, there will be one that will accept dogs.

Sunshine Mission is a red brick building, built around

1910, with graffiti all over it. You'd be hard pressed to find a brick that doesn't have the mark of a "street artist." Behind a metal desk in a dimly lit office sits a man in his sixties who looks like a bulldog.

"What can I do for you?"

"I'd like to rent a room for a month."

"You married?"

I have not been asked this question in years. Grinning, I admit, "No."

"It's just you alone?" He's awfully persistent.

"Yes," I say.

"I charge double for two." He doesn't believe me.

"It's me and my dogs."

Lifting a pencil to a piece of paper, he asks, "Small or large?"

"Both."

"Where are they?"

"With relatives. I'll bring them back here later. Is that okay?"

"If they are well behaved, it should be mighty fine by me." He grabs his chest. "I have a soft spot right here for anything with four legs, including elephants." He hands me a key. "Room twelve. Second floor. Bathroom is in the hall, and it's shared with three other rooms."

"Thank you, sir. Thank you. I must be going."

"In such a hurry, you are."

I walk toward the smudged glass exit. He follows me out.

"You're not going to see the room before you take it?"

"No, I haven't the time."

"It's clean."

"I believe you." I hope he doesn't become a pain.

"I'm Leroy Brown. What's your name?"

"Miss Pink."

Smiling warmly, he says, "Nice to meet you."

"Likewise," I say, a bit thrown off by his unexpected friendliness.

I slip away and sprint up the crowded streets in my new shoes, trying to beat time. "I'll make it, I'll make it, I'll make it," I chant to myself. I have no money left to buy a subway ticket. I can barely move by the time I get uptown. I drag my blistered feet through the front gate, hoping to find a human behind the glass door. The lights are off. I bang on the door, but no one answers. I'm so angry. I thought I had this planned out perfectly. I kick the cement and curse at myself. "You're a stupid, stupid woman!" I say out loud. Then I realize that instead of punishing myself, I should be feeling grateful for everything I have received in my life.

Thank you for giving the dogs a place to sleep and food to eat, and for their future homes. Thank you for Sheila's kindness and competence and understanding. Thank you for Mrs. Wolf's diamonds. Thank you for my new job at the pet store, and for Leroy Brown at the rooming house. Thank you for my health.

Saying these words of gratitude helps to calm me down, but they do nothing for the bleeding blisters on my heels. I can't take off my new sneakers because broken glass is strewn all over the sidewalk. Step by agonizing step, I make it to the park. I now dread sleeping in the park without the dogs, but I'm in no condition to walk in and out of coffee shops all night, so I go to my familiar area where I can hide in the bushes.

After I take off my new sneakers and rub my feet, I gaze up at the well-traveled stars. There are so many that they look like one massive, glittering mess. I understand very little about cosmology, but it's easy to believe in the Big Bang Theory tonight. All I know for sure is that I'm giving up on "should have" and "could have." There is only the here and now.

I carry in my bag a sheet that I put on the ground to prevent my clothes from getting dirty. I use my sweater as a blanket and my purse as a pillow and shut my eyes. I feel bugs crawling on my body. Each time I brush them off, they come back again. Eventually, I accept their company and fall asleep.

● ● ●

I awake just before sunrise and say aloud to myself: "Today is another opportunity to make myself useful." My feet are swollen and it is hard to put on my sneakers. I take deep breaths and stand up. I head to the exit of the park, wincing with each step at first, but soon forgetting the pain.

I wait at the front door of the animal control center until a volunteer arrives and unlocks it. I hurry to the kennel area in back, where my dogs are. Athenia is not in her cage. I frantically search around but she's not anywhere.

Terrified, I run to the overzealous volunteer and demand, "Where is she?"

"Who?"

I grab her by her arm and say in my most serious voice, "If that vet killed her because you told him she is untrained,

125

you'll be sorry."

"I didn't do anything!"

"You think because you're young you'll always be in demand, never disposable like the dogs you condemn. But age is the great equalizer. All skin wrinkles, eventually. Lines will form around your mouth, your breasts will sag to your waist, and your belly will roll over your waistline. You just wait."

Her mouth drops open and her eyes water.

The other volunteers gather around, looking at me as if I've lost my sanity. They don't know what to say.

Sheila rushes in. I'm leaning against a wall for support. The thought of a needle being injected into Athenia's soft, defenseless body because of a piss problem makes me feel faint.

Sheila is annoyed. "If you had arrived on time, none of this would have happened."

"You killed her because I was late?"

"No, it's not what you think. She cried so much I had to take her home. She's in reception, eating."

"She's in there?"

"Yes."

"You scared the daylights out of me."

"I went to see my aunt, who's in the hospital again. You promised me you'd be here before closing. From now on, you will play by the rules. I won't keep breaking them for you."

"Oh Sheila, I'm so sorry."

"Say sorry to her." She points to the overzealous, freaked-out volunteer.

"I'm sorry. I overreacted. It will never happen again. Please forgive me," I sincerely plead.

Now that the volunteer feels safe, she blurts out, "You have a problem and you need to take care of it and stop taking it out on me."

"You're absolutely correct," I agree. Satisfied that she's been given respect, she quiets down and stays close to Sheila.

"Sheila, now that I have a place to live, give me five more dogs before they're exterminated."

"It's expensive to feed and take care of so many. Do you think you can handle it? You just started your job."

"Yes."

One of the volunteers who just witnessed our earlier drama quietly comes from the back carrying a malnourished greyhound.

"He can barely walk. He was found in a basement in Queens," Sheila says.

Another volunteer brings me Athenia.

"You sweet thing," I say, taking Athenia in my arms. "Sheila spared you."

I hug Athenia and she pees. No one says a word. I then pet the shy, cowering greyhound and wipe up Athenia's urine. "I'll take him and Mr. Bull and Blacky, and of course this little one. Soon I'll be able to buy food and shelter for hundreds."

"Yeah, right," Sheila says.

"You don't believe me because you think I have nothing."

"Miss Pink, I know you have everything except money."

"I have that too." I open up Blacky's and Mr. Bull's cages and they jump out and chase each other and lick my new sneakers. "Hello, boys. You are free."

We go to the reception area to say our good-byes when we see the young blonde-haired woman who brought Athenia here the other day. She is walking toward the entrance.

"Oh shit," Sheila says.

"We're hiding in the back. Whistle when she's gone," I tell Sheila.

I gently drag Athenia and the others into the kennel area, and shut the door just enough to hear everything but remain out of sight. I can see a sliver of her blonde hair and a bitten fingernail as she nervously twirls a strand. Athenia can either smell or hear her former owner and is whimpering.

"Don't make a peep," I tell Athenia, but she can't help herself.

"My name is Cindy and I want my dog."

Sheila, always the professional, states the facts: "There are many dogs here. Which one?"

"My ex-boyfriend brought her in the other day. Her name is Lilly. She's a little, feminine, beige mutt."

So her name is Cindy and Athenia's is Lilly.

"She's not here anymore."

Cindy is terrified. "Why not?"

"What do you think happens when you leave dogs here? Do you think they all have happy endings?"

Cindy starts to cry. "Bill said this was a no-kill place."

"He's a liar."

"Oh my God," she wails.

"Cindy, calm down, your dog is in good hands," Sheila says.

"Thank God, thank God. Where is she?"

"She has a new home."

"Where?"

"A loving home."

"I'm her home."

"Listen, I know who she's with. You should be grateful and relieved that she didn't go through the hell that some of these others do. Especially because she's totally untrained."

"She's trained."

"Don't bullshit me. We all know her very well. I can describe the scent of her piss."

"My ex-boyfriend said he was taking her for a walk, and when I came home she was not there."

"That's a lie. I saw you outside. I didn't see you make any effort to stop him from dumping her. Anyway, this is all pointless because it's too late. She's been adopted by Miss Pink, who loves her."

"So do I."

Sheila opens envelopes and stacks letters in piles, then blows her nose. "I won't offer you another dog."

"I don't want another dog. I want mine back. I'll die without her."

"You should've thought of that before."

"I know, I was wrong. I admit it. But I left my boyfriend and I'm here to make amends."

"Not my problem."

"Even criminals have trials," Cindy pleads.

Sheila just looks at her.

"I have nobody and nothing. I'm alone." Cindy is crying hysterically now.

"Calm down or I'm going to have to ask you to leave,"

Sheila says.

Cindy gets on her knees. "I beg you, if I could just talk to that Pink woman—"

"She's very busy."

"What's her cell phone number? I can call her and arrange a time to meet—at her convenience, of course."

"If you want to talk to her, you can come here early mornings before 8:30 a.m. or very late before closing."

"Will she be here later?"

"Possibly. I never know."

"I'll be here."

"Whatever you want. It's your life."

"I'll be back."

"Take your time," Sheila says.

Cindy, sniffling, drags her feet to the front door and turns back to Sheila. "I'm sorry for being stupid and weak. Please forgive me and think about giving me back my Lilly." Then she pushes the front door open and runs out.

I slowly open the kennel door. The reception area is teeming with new volunteers waiting to speak to Sheila.

"My God, what a regretful young woman," I remark to Sheila as she calls off a list of names, starting with "Linda."

"Present."

Handing Linda a clipboard and pen, Sheila instructs her to fill out the form. Before calling out the next name, she says to me, "I'm not so sure about that."

"She really seems to care about Athenia," I say.

"How can you trust the judgment of anyone who would sleep with that creep with the big ears?"

"She wasn't the first woman to make a bad choice, and

she won't be the last. We are all guilty on that score."

"Miss Pink, if she really loves her dog, she'll come back with great humility and beg me again. Then she'll fight you for her."

"Fight me?"

"You are now her enemy."

I'm suddenly reminded of my husband's girlfriend, who called our apartment daily until he finally left me for her.

"Look at the time," I say, switching gears. "Sally will kill me if I'm late."

"Ask your boss if I can get a collar like Athenia's in human size. It's beautiful."

"It's from the new Diamonds Are Forever product line."

"You can't imagine the attention her collar got when I carried her to my apartment."

"I'm glad it's a hit. My boss knows what sells. Look, Sheila, I have one more favor and then I won't ask again."

"What?"

"Can you lend me ten dollars? I'll pay you back tenfold within a few days."

She hands me what I have asked for.

"Thank you, thank you. I just can't walk today."

"I can see the back of your sneaker is bloody."

After leashing up the dogs, I approach several taxis before one agrees to let me in with all of them. I have to carry the greyhound because he can't lift his back legs. Blacky, Mr. Bull, and Athenia have no problem. We sit quietly in the backseat and crawl down Fifth Avenue, which has construction vehicles blocking three lanes. We weave in and out of the bus lane, stopping and starting at least fifty times. The dogs sniff and lick the upholstery and gaze out the windows at the bustling city.

Finally, we arrive at 59th Street. I ask the taxi driver to wait outside Mrs. Wolf's prewar limestone building. I ask the friendly doorman to ring Mrs. Wolf. When she answers, I tell her all the dogs are in her lobby, including Princess Athenia with her ice collar. Could she babysit them for the day and meet me at Strawberry Fields later? She agrees and we hang up.

Then I command all the dogs to sit and stay. All but Athenia listen. I scold her, and she forces herself to sit. But when I rush out to the taxi, she follows me and stands by the curb, begging me to take her along. "Go back," I say. She doesn't move. I carry her back into the lobby and ask the doorman to hold her. I get back into the taxi and head downtown to work.

CHAPTER NINE

My second day of work feels better than the first. I'm getting the hang of the routine. Pet shops are very different from shelters. The environment is happier. There are only puppies here and they are cute even when they smell of pee. Finding them homes should be easier too.

The front door opens and a UPS deliveryman dressed in his brown uniform carefully carries in a wooden crate. When I read the words LIVE ANIMALS and HANDLE WITH LOVE written in large, red letters on all four sides, I realize the holes carved out for breathing are way too small.

He smiles at me. "Sign here, please."

"My, my, what do we have here?" I ask as I sign *Miss Pink*. This is not my real name. My birth name is Lena Schwartz. I was born to Jewish parents in the Midwest. My father was first-generation American. His parents were from a shtetl in Russia on the Black Sea. My great-grandfather was the bandleader in the czar's military orchestra. My mother was born to an uneducated tailor from Romania. She was determined to marry well, and indeed my father achieved success in business by starting his own manufacturing company. I, on the other hand, was advised by my high school guidance counselor to marry after graduating high school and not pursue a formal education because I didn't understand algebra. Instead, I attended Ohio State and graduated with a BA, and immediately moved to New York City in the seventies to find my own success in business. Only after leaving the magazine did I shed Lena Schwartz's businesslike demeanor and warm up to life's inherent joys and absurdities. I took to wearing pink, my favorite color, and Sheila dubbed me Miss Pink the first time I arrived to volunteer at the shelter.

But I'm not feeling so joyful right now. Churning in my stomach is the feeling that something is wrong. I quickly pry the box open with the tip of Sally's prized screwdriver, the one she uses to tighten cage hinges. Cuddled in a corner of the box are three beagle pups. Two are terrified, and one is clearly dead.

Sally appears from the storeroom. "Wonderful. My order has arrived."

With a damp tissue I remove the pups' oozing eye mucus, and then I pick up the limp body of the dead one for Sally to see.

"You accepted this shipment without checking the inventory first? Where's the ferret?"

"Poor things, they had to watch their sibling die," I say, ignoring her statement.

She hands me the phone. "Call them right now. You tell them to pick up all the damaged goods and ship me new ones. I will not be charged for your negligence."

"Where is the telephone number?"

"Can't you see?" Sally points to the red ink. "It's right there on the packing slip."

"Oh yes, it's as clear as an emergency exit sign. Pardon me."

I'm furious at Sally's insensitivity, but I cannot let her get the best of me. These animals need me, so I will do what is best for them by not getting fired. I swallow my anger and dial the number. When someone picks up, I say, "This is Green Pastures Pet Store. May I speak to your shipping department?" I can barely make out what the lady on the other end is saying. As I strain to listen, Sally is hovering over my shoulder and shaking her finger like a crazy woman.

"She's telling me she has no power to make accounting changes," I tell Sally.

She snatches the phone from my hand. "I want to speak to Bob. You know, your boss, the manager." She pauses, impatiently twirling her short blonde hair between two manicured fingers. "I don't care how long I have to wait. Get him on the phone pronto." She pauses again and kicks the wall with one of her black ballet slippers. "He's not in! How long did it take for you to figure that out? Don't talk to me anymore, just have him call me back. . . . My assistant already told you, we're calling from Green Pastures." She slams the phone down on the counter so hard it bounces off and falls on the floor. I bend down to pick it up.

Sally sighs with exasperation. "I do hope they pass stricter immigration laws soon. Nobody speaks English anymore. This is really getting out of hand. Clean up the pups and put them there." She points to the front window. "Oh, and make sure you put a half-price sale sign on the window."

"Where do you want this sweet little soul buried?"

"Wrap him in plastic. I want to return him."

I do what she orders and then pick up the other two sickly pups. Their eyes are barely open and their little pink tongues search my skin for intimacy. They both fit in one hand. "Their eyes need antibiotics," I say. "Infections are contagious. I don't want them to infect the others."

"Maybe we'll sell them both today at a good price and come out ahead."

"They are not healthy," I tell her.

"The customers don't know that."

"They need a doctor."

"That is their owner's responsibility."

As if on cue, the front door opens and a young, perky, dark-haired couple walks in. The woman is seven months pregnant.

Sally strides up to them and says, "Good morning. And how are the two of you on this sunny day?"

"Better, now that the heat has lifted," the pregnant lady says.

"Oh yes, we were under one heck of a spell," Sally agrees.

"Perhaps you can help us," the young man says. "We are looking for a puppy to raise with our newborn."

"You've come to the right place. Many young couples come in here looking for the right puppy. It's important that the temperament of a breed match the family's personality."

"What breed do you think would be right for us?" the young man asks.

"We have two healthy purebred beagle pups that came in from a top breeder in upstate New York. Some of Bob's beagles have won prestigious dog shows. Your timing is perfect. They just arrived this morning." Sally goes to the front window and takes out the one with less mucus in his eyes. "Now is he cute or what?" She hands it off to the pregnant woman, who cradles it and mumbles words of affection. She lovingly offers it to her husband, who also holds the puppy with tenderness.

"I love beagles. We had one when I was a girl."

"They are my favorite breed!" Sally says with practiced enthusiasm.

"It would be wonderful to raise our child with a beagle. Wouldn't it, sweetie?" She looks to her husband for final approval.

Gazing at his wife with affection, he says, "Let's do it, hon."

She hugs him and smiles at Sally. "We are beyond fortunate. Thank you."

"I agree, nothing completes a home like a new dog," Sally quips, "except new curtains."

The couple decides not to respond.

Without further ado, Sally proceeds to the register. "Cash or credit?"

The young man takes out his credit card and hands it to Sally.

"I can ship the dog to New Jersey and save you the hefty New York sales tax."

"No, that's not necessary," he says.

"Oh, but it is. A young couple like you should save money when possible."

"We'd much rather take him home ourselves. We live here in the city."

Sally briefly pats the beagle's head and says, "So, little one, congratulations on your new home."

The young woman asks her husband, "What should we

name him?"

"How about Lucky?" Sally offers, handing the credit card slip to the young man to sign.

"Too obvious," he says as he signs and hands the pen and slip back to Sally. She twirls the pen triumphantly like a mini-baton between two fingers. The man kisses his wife and they both kiss their new beagle.

"I'm so excited. Thank you, honey." The pregnant woman hugs her husband.

I smile at them. What a sweet young family they make. If my ex-husband and I had adopted a puppy together, we might have tried harder to work things out and stay together.

After they leave, I clean the cages and feed the puppies. Soon they are all sleeping. I examine the infected eye of the remaining beagle pup. It is oozing puss. Sally inspects the cages with hardly a glance at the puppies, and then plants herself in front of the computer screen. She stays there all day, never getting up to eat or use the bathroom. I mop and rinse the floor behind the counter several times. Mouse droppings are everywhere again. Tomorrow I'll find the holes and plug them up. The mice are stealing the dog food.

At the end of the day, Sally says good-bye and leaves me to close up shop. I do my final walk-through and clean the beagle pup's eye again. I'll have to find a way to get him medicine without Sally knowing.

● ● ●

I'm happy to be reunited with my dogs at Strawberry Fields, but surprised to find Mrs. Wolf dressed as a homeless man. She is wearing a pair of stained, baggy pants, mismatched socks torn at the ankles, and a Yankees baseball cap atop her usually perfectly coiffed head. She looks like a Charlie Chaplin character and I laugh at the thought of us looking like an odd homeless couple as we walk along the bridal path. It's a glorious night, the temperature is a breezy seventy-eight, and the scent of flowers lingers in the air.

"Your outfit is a trip," I tell Mrs. Wolf.

"My husband's Armani pants are good for something. I had to dirty them to make me less noticeable. The press and the Feds didn't recognize me."

She points to the dogs' necks. Each one is wearing a sparkling diamond collar.

"Holy shit, what are you going to do with them?"

"We need to bury the jewels somewhere we'll both remember. My memory is not what it used to be."

"This sounds risky. Why should I help you?"

"Once everything cools off, I'll be able to sell them."

"What about all those people your husband robbed? Don't they deserve compensation?"

"So you don't believe his fund crashed? We lost most of our money too. Do I have to say it again? Between the Feds and the crash, the jewelry is all I have left, so there won't be enough to go around. Be moralistic if you choose, but once my husband is granted a retrial, let a jury decide who deserves what."

"Over there the ground is softer," I say.

We walk over to the chosen spot and scan the area for people. We're the only ones there. I start to unclasp the "collars" as she explains to me where she bought each necklace and how much she paid. She asks me if I own any fine jewelry. I tell her no, never have, and probably never will.

For the first time I notice a pair of diamond hoop earrings attached to one of the necklaces. When I go to unfasten them, Mrs. Wolf says, "Those were my tenth anniversary present. Leave them."

When I start to take off Athenia's necklace, Mrs. Wolf orders, "Leave it. I can get that one sold in a few days. I have a discreet buyer."

We replace the other diamond necklaces with ordinary collars. I hand Mrs. Wolf the necklaces and she wraps them around her neck while singing "Diamonds Are a Girl's Best Friend," which Marilyn Monroe famously sang in *Gentlemen Prefer Blondes*. I saw the film when I was a young woman and have forgotten most of the lyrics. Mrs. Wolf knows every word.

"Shh," I tell her, nervous that we're being too conspicuous. It would've been safer to smuggle the diamonds out in our pockets, but Mrs. Wolf is obviously enjoying the ceremony.

"I wish I had a bottle of champagne so I could make a toast to you, a kindred soul."

"I'm not a kindred soul."

"Oh, I think you are."

"I've worked for my money."

"Mazel tov, so have I."

"Shh, I think I hear somebody." I'm lying, but it does the trick. She is silent.

She takes out from a thick paper bag a small, sharp shovel. She struggles to bend down to the ground with it.

"I have arthritis in my knee." This must be why she never picked up after her dog.

I take the shovel from her and proceed to dig a deep hole. By the time I'm finished, Mrs. Wolf has taken all the diamonds from her neck and tucked them lovingly back in the purple velvet satchel and the black plastic bag. I lay the bag of goods in the hole.

"Diamonds will outlive us all," Mrs. Wolf says.

"So will our reputations," I say.

"If you're still judging me, I'm not offended. I understand your ambivalence."

I fill the hole with dirt and mark the spot with a small, yellowish rock.

"What a magnificent evening. I can't remember when I last felt so refreshed," Mrs. Wolf enthuses.

"The breeze feels good," I say, trying to be agreeable.

Exhausted, I take a seat on the ground, and she joins me, first lowering herself gingerly on her knees and then plopping herself all the way down like an anchor. The dogs have already made themselves comfortable near us.

"We're just like hens sitting on our eggs, waiting for them to hatch," she says.

"Delusions of grandeur, my dear. We can't reproduce at this age," I reply.

"Well, truth be told, I never could. At any age."

Sitting near the small covered hole, watching the sun sink toward the west, Mrs. Wolf begins to describe her husband and their tumultuous marriage. He left her several times for younger women but always came back. She regrets not being able to have children. She tried many times, but it never worked. I understand her regret because I went through a similar experience, even tried IVF. My eggs were just too weak or too old. Listening to her brings back too many heavy memories. Under their weight, I feel compelled to lie flat on my back. The dogs, seeming to sense my mood, huddle closer to me. Abigail joins us.

"Abby, I'm not chopped liver. Come back here," Mrs. Wolf says, feeling a twinge of betrayal. Her sheltie begrudgingly gets up to sit beside her, but when Mrs. Wolf is not looking Abby inches slowly back toward my clan.

"My whole life, I wanted Elizabeth Taylor diamonds," Mrs. Wolf recalls. "My husband worked hard to give me what I wanted. If only I could have stayed in the railroad flat on First Avenue when we were first married and not demanded more and more of him, he wouldn't have taken all those risks."

"As long as you make peace with yourself, that is all that matters," I offer.

"Obviously I'm not at peace with anything, especially not with having to live my worst fears."

"Resisting it won't make it better."

"If you were ugly like me you'd resist it, believe me, and you would do everything you could to change it."

"You are not ugly," I protest, surprised at this turn in the conversation.

"You can say that because you are naturally pretty. Look at you—no wrinkles. And your nose looks like a Dr. Diamond special. It's perfect, not like my huge shnoz. It takes a lot of money to make me attractive."

"That's not true."

"I'm not weak. I can handle the truth."

"The truth is, we'd all be better off trying to be more like them," I say, gesturing to Athenia, Mr. Bull, Blacky, Abby, and the greyhound. "You think they worry about their noses, or what carat diamonds they're wearing around their necks? All they need to feel like a million bucks is love and affection."

"Easy for them, they're dogs. Besides, dogs aren't ugly like most people are. But okay, maybe I'm not ugly—just homely, like my mother used to say."

There is nothing more I want to say to her. The subject of looks is tiring. I gaze at the sky, which has gotten all peachy with the sunset. Nature is always beautiful. It's just that mankind has lost touch with it.

Realizing that I'd rather change the subject, Mrs. Wolf calmly asks, "So Miss Pinky, what are you going to do with your cut of the jewels?"

"Buy homes," I say, not bothering to correct her on my name.

"You're worse than I am. How many homes do you need?"

"Not for me, for the dogs."

"I can help you. You'll need to create a nonprofit to do that. Get a board together, and a budget—you know, just like the big boys."

"Just you and me. No big boys. And I don't want anyone to know about the diamonds."

"Well then, I have a wonderful attorney. You can use him. He does pro bono for certain causes and he can keep a secret."

"How much money are we talking about?" I ask her.

"If you can help me get all the jewels out of my place, it's about five million bucks. I'll give you half of that."

"How much did we just bury?"

"Half a million."

"I'll need some of it tomorrow."

"Not possible. I have to sell them first."

"Meet me at the animal control center tomorrow, same time." I stand up and brush myself off.

"The night is still young. Why are you rushing off?"

"I need to feed these guys and get to the rooming house."

"I fed them already."

"I still want to go."

"Give me one more minute. I haven't sat on the grass in years. I feel like a teenager again. Have you ever slept in the park?"

"No," I lie.

"It could be fun."

"Sleep here and I'll come for you tomorrow."

"Me, sleep in the park? What would people say?"

"It may work to your benefit. Think of the *New York Post* headline: 'Rich Wife of Ponzi Investor Now Homeless.' They'll think you got what was coming to you. Their revenge will set you free."

"Help me up, please." She extends her frail arms toward me.

I pull her up. "Easy does it," I say.

She stands hunched over for a moment, trying to straighten up. Slowly, her back erects itself and she shakes blood back into her thin, arthritic legs.

"Okay, let's go," she orders, and we walk through the now dark, half-empty park to the exit. She kisses my cheek good-bye.

I'm not sure if this lady is a good person, but she has a certain openness and charm that may win people over. I hope Sheila agrees with me, because I intend for all of us to work together.

I head home to the rooming house with the dogs and sneak them by Leroy Brown when I spy him getting up to take a bathroom break. He said he likes dogs, but this many? There is no reason to start our landlord-tenant relationship with undue stress. I don't want a repeat of the Madeline situation.

Once in the room, I take off my sneakers, run cold water on a washcloth, and drape it around my sore feet. Somehow, I made it through the day by forgetting the pain. Come to think of it, that's a very powerful concept, perhaps worth sharing with Mrs. Wolf. I'll tell her that if she doesn't like her face, she should stop looking in the mirror.

The dogs surround me and kiss my feet. They know they are loved and lie content on and around the bed in their temporary home. Athenia has another one of her running dreams. Her paws move faster than a conveyer belt. In the morning I walk each one separately, then return them to my room. Leroy doesn't seem to mind me going in and out with a different dog every twenty minutes. His only comment is "Are you the local dog walker?" I reply with a smile.

● ● ●

I put in an exhausting day at the pet shop—exhausting because Sally sucks up my energy like a vampire. Then I go to see Sheila. She's stacking small packages in piles. The keys and her purse are on the desk. She's ready to lock up. I'm wondering where Mrs. Wolf is.

Sheila has a strange expression. "She was here again."

"Who?"

"Athenia's mother, Cindy, who comes and cries in the reception area and won't leave me alone. One of the board members happened to be here and overheard her endless pleading and asked me why I wouldn't give her dog back. I told her that Athenia was adopted. The board member felt sorry for Cindy and strongly suggested that we call the person who adopted the young lady's dog and explain the desperate situation. Then I got a call from the girl's father, who apparently is one of our pro bono lawyers, and he demanded we give back the dog."

"I thought her father didn't want the dog and that is why she went to live with the boyfriend."

"I don't care about their *Peyton Place*. I just know I'm being politically pressured by the powers that be."

"Let me think about it."

"That means no. I know you by now, Miss Pink."

"Will you do me a favor? At the pet shop, there is a sick beagle with an eye infection. Can you give me a tube of antibiotic cream?"

"You know all the medicine is locked up in the back."

"Can you unlock the cabinet?"

"As you know, I'm not allowed to treat dogs that aren't residents in the shelter."

"Can we make an exception?"

Sheila considers for a moment, then relents. "Don't tell anyone."

"I'll pay you back when I get paid."

We walk back to the kennel area where the walls are shaking with the desperate wailing. I dream of buying a warehouse and converting it to many small homes for these unfortunate souls. I'd hire Sheila to manage it.

We hear a knock on the front door.

"Oh shit, I hope it's not another animal being dumped," Sheila says.

Another knock.

We walk to the reception area, and standing outside in the dark, without her baseball cap but still in homeless garb, is Mrs. Wolf.

"I know her. I can't place it, but we've met before," Sheila says.

"Where?" I ask.

"It will come to me." The face she makes is one of bewilderment and suspicion.

"Did you see her dumping a sheltie?"

"No, the old sheltie was brought in by a fat, middle-aged, balding man."

"Oh good, so she wasn't lying."

"What do you mean?"

"Nothing."

I unlock the door. Mrs. Wolf steps in with Abigail, whose neck is draped with a diamond necklace.

"You're late. Sheila, meet—"

"Mrs. Abigail," Mrs. Wolf says.

"Nice to meet you." She shakes Mrs. Wolf's delicate, age-spotted hand. Her nails are impeccably manicured with light silver polish.

"I brought this for you." Mrs. Wolf takes the collar off Abigail and hands it to me.

"Sheila, you take it," I say, handing over the necklace to her.

Mrs. Wolf stomps her feet. "Miss Pink, I bought it for your mutt."

"It will look better on Sheila."

"I don't think so," Mrs. Wolf says.

"Why not?" Sheila interjects.

Sheila drapes the long strand around her own neck. "How beautiful. Are you sure you didn't get this from Harry Winston?"

"No, I got it from the pet store. Second row on the right side," Mrs. Wolf says.

Sheila can't take her eyes off Mrs. Wolf. She studies every square inch of her. "I was telling Miss Pink how familiar you look," Sheila says to her.

"Must be my common face. "

There's a knock on the door. We all look over to see who it is. It's Cindy. When Sheila opens the door, Cindy falls at her feet, crying, "Please, where is the Pink lady?"

"I'm the Pink lady. What can I do for you?"

She moans, "My dog, my dog, I need her back!"

Mrs. Wolf says, "Calm down, young lady. You're giving me a headache."

"Mrs. Wolf—I mean, Mrs. Abigail—that comment is not necessary. Let this young lady express herself," I say.

Sheila says, "I agree with your friend. It's giving me a headache, too."

"Maybe Pinky is right," Mrs. Wolf says. "We should be more compassionate. The young woman is obviously very upset."

Sheila rolls her eyes in annoyance.

I tell Cindy, "Tomorrow night, at this time, meet me here and we'll talk about what you have to do to get your dog back. Sheila, please excuse us." Then I grab Mrs. Wolf by the hand to escort her out.

Cindy kisses me on my cheek and says, "I'll be here. Thank you so much for listening. Thank you."

As I make my way with Mrs. Wolf to the door, Sheila whispers in my ear, "I thought you were straight."

"I am."

"Don't get me wrong, I'm happy for you."

"What's that supposed to mean?"

"Excuse us," Sheila says to Mrs. Wolf and Cindy, pulling me into the back room. "What's the attitude about?" she asks me.

"You have been making strange faces at Mrs. Abigail. It's rude."

"There's something not right about her. I can't put my finger on it."

"There's nothing to figure out."

"Yes, there is."

I walk back into the reception area, and Sheila follows.

"Is everything okay?" Mrs. Wolf asks, searching my eyes for an answer. I reveal nothing.

"Yes," Sheila responds.

Cindy has finally stopped crying and says, "My father said I could come here and get my dog back."

"You have to earn her back," I say.

"I'll do whatever you want." She smiles sweetly, asking for forgiveness.

Could Cindy be one of us? A true animal lover like Sheila, Mrs. Wolf, and me? I file this thought away for later.

"Ladies, let's wrap this up tomorrow," Sheila says. "I'm exhausted."

"Everything is settled. Cindy will get her dog back," I say.

"Oh, Miss Pink, thank you. I'll tell my dad everything worked out," Cindy happily offers.

"If you or anyone associated with you dumps a pet again, you'll be held accountable to a higher source," I say.

"I promise it won't happen again," Cindy says, and waits until I signal with a nod that I've accepted her promise. She's just like Athenia: sweet, defenseless, eager to please.

Sheila turns off the lights and Cindy lingers behind Mrs. Wolf as we exit the front door. Outside, Sheila seems relieved to say goodnight and to head home. Once she's gone, I ask Cindy, "Do you know how to groom animals?"

"No."

"Learn, as fast as possible. I have work for you."

"Really? That's wonderful!" Cindy says.

She tries to tag along with me and Mrs. Wolf, but we ignore her. "What are you two doing tonight?" she asks us.

"We have some work to do. See you tomorrow," I say.

After another block, I turn to find her still following behind. She gives a little jump, as if caught doing something wrong, and says, "Sorry, I was just going this way." She quickly crosses the street and disappears around the corner.

"Lonely young woman," I say to Mrs. Wolf.

"I can't imagine why, though. She's quite pretty."

Mrs. Wolf and I head through the dark, abandoned park to monitor if our necklaces are still safely buried.

Mrs. Wolf says, "Imagine a rapist lurking in the tunnel over there."

"Don't you see the locked gate at the entrance? No one can hide in there."

"Goodness!" she screams.

"What is it?"

"Something just ran over my foot."

"Don't worry, it's probably just a mouse."

"I pay all these taxes and there are still rodents in the park. What happened to the traps?"

"Those are for rats."

"Rats!"

"They are shy. You're safe."

"You sure?"

"Yes."

When we get to the hole, I realize it looks freshly dug and easily detectable, so I throw more leaves on top. Mrs. Wolf is still angry that I gave Sheila the necklace and rants on about where she bought it and how much she paid.

"I don't care to hear about where or how much," I tell her. "It's just a pretty necklace, and Sheila deserves it more than most."

"But Miss Pinky, that necklace—"

"If you persist in boring me with details, I will not help you," I state firmly.

She shuts up and we continue quietly to the East 72nd Street exit. We hear shuffling. We stop. The shuffling stops.

"We're in trouble," Mrs. Wolf says. "I left my gun in the other purse."

"Why would you carry a gun?"

"To defend myself, why else?"

We hear the sound again. It's getting closer.

"Run!" I say. We take off like bandits and make it to the exit without turning back. When we finally turn back, we find a miniature Yorkie has followed us and is begging to be picked up. We laugh at our own foolishness.

"Unbelievable," Mrs. Wolf says as she tries to catch her breath.

I pick up the harmless creature and continue to walk.

"He must have been left here. There's no tag." I cuddle the shaking Yorkie. His fur is matted and muddy. We head across town on East 72nd Street.

"Beautiful townhouses on this block," Mrs. Wolf observes.

"I thought we were going down to the Bowery."

"I need to make a pit stop."

"How far?"

"We're here."

We stop mid-block at a doorman building. The garbage is neatly piled in front of the service entrance, and neatly folded in a clear plastic bag are several women's pants suits. I unzip the bag and examine the clothes.

"How did you know the clothes would be here?"

"The lady who lives in 24B often leaves stuff she's only worn a few times. I have to get here at a certain hour before someone else picks it up."

There is a lovely pink pants suit a couple sizes too large for me, but I can take in the pants and wear layers under the linen jacket.

"Do you see anything you like?"

"No, I'm afraid I've developed a dislike of suits. Baggy men's pants are much more comfortable."

I put the pants suit in my purse, along with the little dog, and we head to the Bowery. The Yorkie sniffs everything with his little wet nose.

When Mrs. Wolf and I arrive at the rooming house, Leroy Brown is eating a large hamburger covered in ketchup and pickles. Leroy's hands are large enough to hold it neatly in one piece. He looks up and smiles at us.

"This is where I live," I tell Mrs. Wolf.

"Too bad for you."

"This is where you could live, if you don't want to live with your sister-in-law."

"I wouldn't dare."

"The press won't look for you here."

"Avoiding them keeps me occupied. I've got nothing else to do."

"Then help me rescue dogs."

The small TV on the reception desk is blaring music. Leroy's eyes are glued to the screen. When he sees us he puts his hamburger down and wipes his fingers. "I love reality shows—anybody can be a star! Hello, Miss Pink," he exclaims good-naturedly and shakes my hand.

"Hi, Mr. Brown. This is my coworker, Mrs. Wolf."

"I'm just a friend. Far from a coworker."

"Pleasure to meet you, whoever you are," he says.

"You wouldn't want to know."

"If you put it like that." Turning to me, he says, "Your many creatures of the universe are very sweet."

"You met them?"

"I had the pleasure. I'm not supposed to enter a boarder's room unless there is a problem, but I used my passkey when I heard crying."

"Oh, so there was a problem?"

"Not for me, but your neighbors complained. Don't worry. If they don't like it here, they can leave."

"Thank you, Mr. Brown. If there is anything I can do for you, like loan you money or something, let me know."

"You? Loan him money?" Mrs. Wolf asks incredulously.

"How much we talkin'?" he asks with a rakish grin that tells me he's not taking me seriously.

"Whatever you need."

Trying not to smile, he says, "Ten thousand."

"It's yours, just wait a few months."

"Yeah, sure." He laughs.

"I'm telling the truth."

"You're a nice person, and I know you would if you could."

"Good evening, sir."

"Good evening, ladies. If your girlfriend's staying the night, I won't charge double like I normally do."

"She's not," I say.

At the stairs, Mrs. Wolf whispers that Leroy has a crush on me.

"Mind your own business," I tell her.

"Don't underestimate the importance of companionship."

"The dogs give me all the companionship I need, Mrs. Wolf."

"I understand. I love my Abbie, too, but a dog can't substitute for a man."

"We have a bit of a climb up these old stairs. Hold on to the railing and pull yourself up if it gets to be too much."

"I can handle it if the steps aren't too steep."

We nearly make it to the third floor when Mrs. Wolf pauses. I get behind her and push her up the remaining three steps.

"Thank you. My knee needs to be replaced."

The hallway is clean and well lit. My room is all the way at the end, in the corner. The wooden door is freshly painted white. The room is about twenty by fifteen feet, with large windows on both sides for cross ventilation and a ceiling fan. There are two single beds with sheets and pillowcases, two towels, a hot plate, and a small new rug in the bathroom. The room is freshly painted shiny pink and the floor is cement. Leroy even put several pieces of fruit on a paper plate with a note saying welcome.

"He painted the room pink. Imagine that," I say.

"What did I tell you?"

The dogs are ecstatic to see us and sniff the Yorkie as I put him on the floor. They jump up on us as if starved for human companionship. I have to command them to get down. When I sit on the bed, Athenia hops up with me, and Blacky and Mr. Bull hop on the other one. The greyhound can't jump, so he curls up on the hard floor near my bed. Mrs. Wolf paces, and Abby and the Yorkie follow her back and forth across the room.

"Sleep with them on the other bed, or on the floor, or wherever you want."

"I don't know what to do anymore. I've slept on ten-thousand-dollar mattresses and now I'm reduced to these inhumane conditions. If only he hadn't lost all that money."

"If you think this is inhumane, you haven't spent enough time in the kennel. Tell me, Mrs. Wolf, what's the worst thing that can happen to you?"

"Let's start with no new clothes."

"Wrong. Next."

"Living in a dump."

"Being paralyzed by fear. Conquer your fear, that's the goal."

"How?"

"Recognize when maintaining the status quo is more painful than making a change."

"I don't know how you do it, Miss Pinky, living like you do day in and day out."

"I'm better off today than I was last week," I say.

"How can you justify your life?"

"Find something to do that makes you feel worthwhile."

"You make it sound so easy, but it's all just self-help nonsense. It's giving me a headache." Mrs. Wolf takes off her socks and lies down in the middle of the other bed, with Blacky and Mr. Bull on either side of her feet. Abigail remains on the floor with the grateful greyhound, and the tiny Yorkie curls up inside Mrs. Wolf's shoe.

Mrs. Wolf pats the bed. "Get your butt up here, Abby." Abigail stays put. "Stupid girl, I won't feed you if you don't do as I say."

Abigail jumps up onto the bed between Blacky and Mr. Bull and lays her head on one of Mrs. Wolf's bare feet.

Mrs. Wolf sits up to pet Abigail's forehead. "My toes are ugly," she observes.

Like perfect gentlemen, Mr. Bull and Blacky take this as their cue to jump off the bed, giving Mrs. Wolf and Abigail personal space.

Before long, we all fall asleep. But Mrs. Wolf turns out to be an Academy Award-winning snorer, and throughout the night Athenia and I are startled awake by her loud, choking moans. Eventually, I have to go to her bed and shake her. "Mrs. Wolf, Mrs. Wolf, wake up."

"What's wrong?"

"You're snoring."

"I hope I'm not disturbing you."

"Turn over on your stomach."

She does, which helps for a while, but soon she is snoring loudly again.

"Turn on your side," I say.

She rolls over, and Abby jumps off the bed.

Mrs. Wolf's husband is better off in jail. He's probably sleeping more soundly there than he has in years.

CHAPTER TEN

Exhausted, I arrive at the pet shop a half hour early so I can clean the beagle pup's eye with antibiotic ointment. After I'm finished with her, I tend to a sick poodle pup who is throwing up. I clean him and his cage, and then start my rounds of feeding.

The door slams open and the young man who bought the beagle pup yesterday stands there holding the dead puppy and demanding to see the manager.

"Sir, I'm so sorry, the manager will be here shortly."

Sally struts in carrying her Blackberry and a coffee. "Oh, hi, back to extend the family?"

He sticks the pathetic dead puppy in her face. "Do you see? We tried to save him. I took him to the hospital and he died right there on the table." He hands her the limp puppy. "You bury him." She grabs him and places him on the counter as if he's a stuffed animal. He's beginning to smell. "My wife cried all night. I don't like that."

"I'll refund your money. These things do happen. Not often, may I add, but they are living, breathing, organic beings and life is far from perfect."

"I'm so sorry," I say, feeling terrible about the situation.

"Go in the back, Miss Pink. You're not needed here."

I walk into the storage room, leaving the door slightly open so I can hear Sally's lies.

"How could you sell a sick puppy to a pregnant woman? How could you do that to my wife?"

"I didn't do it on purpose. I'll credit your Visa, if that is okay." Sally's tone is indignant.

"It won't take away my family's first tragic loss."

"I'll give you a steep discount on another animal."

"Not from this store."

"Give us another opportunity to make your experience at our store better."

"I think you were fully aware of the dog's condition. I'm going to report you to the Better Business Bureau."

"This is an upstanding pet store. Here, please take this credit refund."

He storms out of the shop.

"Miss Pink, I need your help out here."

I peek my head out. "Yes, Sally, what can I do for you?"

"Tomorrow I want you to work late because I'm returning the sick beagle pup to his breeder. Come here, I'm not going to scream."

I walk up to her and stare into two blank eyes. "He won't make it. He needs medicine now."

"Don't argue with me. Put him in the crate and I'll take him home so I don't have to come here in the morning."

"You mean the crate he came in, the one in the back?"

"I'm not going to use one of my expensive ones."

"The holes are too small in that other crate."

"That's not my problem. As far as I'm concerned, he's damaged merchandise. I'm going to the gym. Have him ready by the time I get back."

Sally hands the dead beagle to me. "Wrap this up and put

it in with the other one. I'm returning both of them."

I nod and she leaves. I take a knife and bore more holes in the crate. That's the least I can do. I pick up the sick beagle and gently place him in there, assuring him he'll be okay. He's completely defenseless. His whimpers make me angry at Sally, at the puppy mill, and at myself for not taking swift enough action.

Although I am not a Christian, I have always loved the Christian teaching of forgiveness and I've tried to practice it throughout my life. But I will be honest: it is not always easy. I still have trouble forgiving my ex-husband for his betrayals. And now I wonder how one is to forgive a sadist like Sally. This, however, is no time for forgiveness. First, I must protect the animals. I decide to return to the sick poodle, take him out of his cage, and hide him behind the stack of dry dog food bags. Customers come in to buy leashes and toys; nobody will notice the hidden puppy.

By the time Sally returns from the gym, I've made seven sales. But I don't care anymore about my sales success, and I certainly don't want Sally to see a penny of it. In her tight black pants, she makes a beeline for the cash register.

"Very good, seven sales." She opens the crate. "If Bob charges extra for damaging his crate, I'll deduct it off your first paycheck."

"You can do that."

"And don't forget to turn off the air conditioner."

"We have to leave the air on low, otherwise it will be too hot for them."

"Energy costs money. I'll take it from your pay."

"I need my pay."

"Listen, I make the rules around here, not you. Got it? We can go over them again when I get back," she snarls, then leaves in a huff.

● ● ●

It's mid-afternoon. I put the closed sign on the door and take the sick poodle with me, leaving the lights and air conditioner on. I don't have enough money to buy a subway ticket, so I walk more than three miles to the Animal Care Center.

Finally, out of breath, I enter carrying the sick little brown poodle puppy under my arm. "Sheila, I don't care anymore if I'm fired, but I have to get the animals out of there."

"What's wrong? You look horrible."

"This little one is dying."

Sheila gets on the phone and asks the vet to come to the reception desk to look at the sick puppy. When he arrives, I'm relieved to see he's not the exterminator. He gently examines the puppy and gives him a shot of medicine. He tells us the puppy has a worm but that he'll feel better in a few days. As the vet goes over a care checklist, Athenia's mother walks into the reception area.

Sheila whispers, "She's been here twice this morning, looking for you."

Cindy smiles and shakes my hand. "How are you, Miss Pink?"

"Fine. You're early. Come with me," I say.

"Where are we going?"

"To a pet store."

"I want my little girl back."

"She's not here. You'll see her after we run this errand."

"But you said I could have her today."

"Is today finished yet?"

"No."

"Then stop complaining."

"I'm sorry."

"Speaking of sorry, what happened to your boyfriend?"

"I left him."

"Why?"

"He doesn't want her living with us."

"And where are you living now?"

"At my father's."

"Athenia is not a yo-yo. She should stay with me until you get your living situation figured out."

"Her name is Lilly."

"We named her Athenia."

"My father said Lilly can stay until I get my own place."

"She goes by Athenia now."

"Okay, Lilly will be her middle name."

"Now that we understand each other, I can offer you an opportunity of a lifetime."

Sheila intervenes. "What are you promising her?"

"A career."

"How so?"

"I'm starting a nonprofit called Dogs Have Angels Too."

"With what money?" Sheila asks.

"Private investors."

"My gut never lies. I knew she was your lover!" Sheila says.

"She's my investor."

"Yeah, right."

"Sheila, thank you so much for helping me out. Do you mind watching the puppy for me until I come back for him later?"

"Miss Pink, you're acting elusive these days."

"I'm sorry you feel that way." I kiss Sheila on the cheek, which is not what I normally do. Her mouth drops wide open.

"I just figured it out. I know who she is," Sheila says.

"Who?"

"She's Ruth Madoff."

"No, she's not."

"How the hell did you hook up with her?"

"Her name is Mrs. Wolf, not Madoff."

"Wait, I'll show you."

Sheila goes to her computer and plugs away at the keyboard. Scanning the screen, she says, "You see? Come here." I walk over. She points to her screen. "I told you so."

"That's not her!" I say

"She looks just like her."

"But it's not her."

Sheila rubs her eyes and examines the image again. "Okay, you're right." She clicks and clicks. I stand there, staring at images of smiling women dressed in white linen and jewels at local South Hampton charity events. Then she stops. "Wait a minute, there she is, standing next to Madoff at another party. That's her, look."

"Yes, that's her," I agree.

"I knew I smelled a rat."

"So they're charity sisters, nothing more," I say dismissively.

Which sends Sheila into a tirade claiming that Mother Teresa was the only person who could be excused for taking from the mob. "You are not Mother Teresa!" she concludes, then adds, "Furthermore, it's bad karma to take blood money."

"Suffering animals don't know the difference."

"Suffering people do."

"I really must be off. I have to get back to the animals."

"Don't take anything from her!" Sheila warns me.

I don't want to ignore Sheila—I have too much respect for her—but I'm in a difficult position and must follow my own conscience. "I'm so sorry that we don't agree. Perhaps one day you will understand my position."

Cindy is watching and listening. She makes an attempt to say something, but I cut her off with a question: "Dear, don't you think you should use the bathroom before we go? It's a four- to five-mile walk, and there won't be time for pit stops on the way."

"I'll be fine, Miss Pink. My father says I've got the bladder of a camel."

I wave good-bye to Sheila, who merely casts me a disappointed look.

We walk downtown to the East Village. Cindy begins to complain about her swollen feet, and I tell her to be quiet, that life is all about overcoming adversity.

When we get to the pet store, I unlock the doors and, as we enter, the animals cry for our attention.

"Please grab the cardboard crates from the back and

bring them up front."

Cindy does as she is told and stacks them near the occupied steel cages. We take out the twelve puppies and place them with toys into two crates. She talks gently to each one.

"It's time to go," I say.

"Where to?"

"My place."

"With all the dogs? But they don't belong to you."

"They are God's creatures. They belong to no one, and that includes Athenia. You are a caretaker, a teacher, a parent. Not the owner of some piece of property. Do you understand?"

"Are you saying you're not going to give me back my dog?"

"They have souls. Our society might buy and sell souls, but they belong to no one."

She asks again, timidly, "Are you giving me back Athenia-Lilly?"

"Yes."

"Then I'll do whatever you want."

"Good, now you can help me carry these puppies, but first take twenty dollars from the cash register. We'll need it for a taxi."

"Will I get into trouble?"

"Not if I return the money later, which I have every intention of doing."

She opens the cash register and reluctantly plucks a twenty from it and slips the money into the back pocket of her blue jeans. Then she holds the door open for me as I carry out the puppy-filled crates. I hit the lights and lock up. It's starting to rain hard and I notice many taxis have gone off duty. Fortunately, one stops right in front of us to drop off an old woman and a young boy. The boy is excited to see all the puppies and asks his grandmother if he can get one. She looks questioningly at me, and I tell them to meet us here at the shop tomorrow so I can help them choose the right one.

The taxi drops us off directly in front of the rooming house. Leroy must be on his break, so I smile at the stranger behind the front desk and we walk right in with our crates of puppies, explaining nothing. When I get to the door, I hear intense barking. When we enter, Cindy almost drops her crate out of excitement. I take it from her as Athenia runs straight up to her, howling and demanding to be picked up. Cindy sweeps her up in her arms and hugs her with tears streaming down her face. "I missed you, my little darling. I love you so much. I promise I'll never leave you again."

"My God, one would think the dog saw an apparition," Mrs. Wolf says.

Cindy is so overwhelmed with emotion she can barely speak.

I open the crates and, one by one, the puppies climb over each other to explore the room. Blacky, Athenia, Mr. Bull, Abby, and the greyhound gently smell each one by way of greeting. The Yorkie observes with curiosity from a safe distance. It occurs to me that if I died at this moment, I'd die happy and surrounded by love.

"It's a madhouse in here. Why do you have so many puppies?" Mrs. Wolf says.

"I rescued them from the pet store."

"Get a load of her blonde locks. You see, Miss Pinky, when you are young, even a bad-hair day looks sexy."

"Growing older and wiser can be sexy, too," I opine.

"Having age spots, rickety knees, and thinning hair is *not* sexy."

"Learning to overcome adversity and accept yourself is."

"Who says any of that comes with age?"

"That's true, some old people don't put up a fight and simply bemoan their fate."

"I hope you aren't referring to me."

"Of course not."

"So, tell me, was there a fire at the store? I mean, why on earth did you bring them here?"

"She was abusing them."

Mrs. Wolf examines the puppies. "Who?"

"The pet store manager."

"They look fine to me, but I'm no expert. Do you have proof?"

"Yes."

"Good, then you should call the ASPCA before the pet shop owners accuse you of stealing their property and have you arrested."

"Cindy, please stay here with the dogs and feed them around five. Mrs. Wolf and I have to go somewhere. We'll be back after dark."

"Is there food here?"

"No."

"Should I buy some?"

"Yes. I'll pay you back."

"You don't have to, Miss Pink. You took good care of Athenia-Lilly. I can see how clean she is, and she even looks like she gained a little weight."

Athenia runs over to me.

"Give me a kiss, little girl. Aren't you a lucky one? And you deserve the best of everything." I start to tear up.

"Don't. You'll make me cry too," Cindy says.

"I just wish they could all have sweet endings like her. Although I'm so happy for you two, I'll be sad to see her go."

"I know," Cindy says, sniffling.

"Now that's enough, girls," Mrs. Wolf interjects. "We're professionals. Professionals don't cry."

Cindy asks, "What kind of professional am I?"

"Whatever you want to be," Mrs. Wolf says.

"A mom," she says.

"You're too young to be a mom," Mrs. Wolf says.

"I don't have to worry about that now," Cindy replies, suddenly sad and pensive.

"The only advice I can offer is do not rush into anything. Besides that, I suggest you cover the whole floor with newspaper for those puppies."

"Yes, Mrs. Wolf."

"The time has come for our rendezvous," Mrs. Wolf says as she tugs at my arm.

"Cindy, thank you very much for helping me out today."

"No problem, Miss Pink."

I say good-bye to all the dogs. Athenia stays glued to Cindy's side. I realize the choice to give her back was the right one.

As I unlock the door to let ourselves out, I tell Mrs. Wolf, "Before we go to the park, I need to pass by the pet store and tell Sally what I did and settle our accounts."

"That should be more entertaining than a Broadway play. You wouldn't happen to have a fresh stick of lipstick? I like to look presentable when I go to the theater."

"No."

"Too bad."

There's a knock on the door.

"Who could that be?" I ask Mrs. Wolf

"How would I know? You're the one who lives here."

Blacky growls, the others bark.

"Who is it?" I ask through the door.

"Leroy Brown, like the song. You fill in the blanks."

Mrs. Wolf smiles mischievously, as if recalling her younger days. "I remember he was the bad man in the town. Sounds like he could have been fun."

I open the door.

"Oh, hello ladies . . ." He looks around. "And hello, animals. I see you have converted the room into a shelter."

"Isn't it wonderful?" I say.

"Yes, we all need homes, but our building isn't licensed for that use."

"I'm sorry. I'll get most of them out of here as soon as possible."

"Miss Pink, if it's temporary there is not a problem. But you forgot to drop the rent off at the front desk like you said you would."

"I'm getting paid today. I'll be back later, and I will give it to you for this week and next."

"Your word is your bond. I will not ask again."

"Thank you, kind sir. And thanks for the fruit and the pink walls."

"I like you. I like what you do. Let's stay friends. Know what I mean?"

"Miss Pink gets the point," Mrs. Wolf says. "You don't have to beat her with it. She's not a dog."

"I apologize if I have offended you, Miss Pink. Good day, ladies."

"No offense taken, and you deserve to be paid. Good day, Mr. Brown," I say.

Mrs. Wolf and I wave good-bye, and he walks away as if just dismissed from the principal's office. The fallen hem on his right pant leg drags on the dusty wooden floor. There is something boyish and vulnerable about this man, despite his bulldog build.

When I close the door again, Mrs. Wolf says, "I did not like the tone he took with you."

"He's a nice man," I say in his defense.

"It was uncalled for. He knows you are borderline homeless."

"I beg your pardon?"

"You are homeless, aren't you?" she asks indignantly.

"May I remind you, I have a bed frame and you do not."

Athenia whines and runs in circles around the room. She is like a carbon monoxide detector for human tension.

Cindy pleads, "Stop arguing, please. You're upsetting her."

"So sorry, dear. We are wasting time with this foolishness, aren't we?" I say.

"That's okay, I understand, Miss Pink." She walks over to me and gives me a huge hug. I let her, and it feels good.

Mrs. Wolf can't stand this show of affection and goes to the window, turning her back to us. "Cindy, will you please take good care of the only family member I have left who is not in a cage?"

"Yes, of course, Mrs. Wolf. Abby is a sweetheart. She's no trouble at all."

We head downstairs into the lobby. Several backpacking Europeans inquire about renting a room for the week. Leroy gazes past them and waves to us as we slip out.

CHAPTER ELEVEN

The mailman couldn't deliver the mail because the shop was closed, so he piled it neatly against the front door. I pick it up and let us in, asking Mrs. Wolf to flip around the closed sign to say we're open. I adjust the air conditioning, open and organize the mail in piles, and clean a few cages as Mrs. Wolf browses the merchandise.

Sally enters carrying a crate filled with beagle pups. Mrs. Wolf pretends she is a customer reading a pet care book.

"Good day, Sally. Did you have a nice trip?"

"Too long." She takes the beagle pups out of the crate, and when she goes to put them in a cage, she realizes all the cages are empty. "What happened to all the merchandise?"

"I took one to the doctor and the others to my home."

"You what?"

"I took them all."

"Did you pay for them?"

"Not yet. But that is why I'm here, to settle our accounts."

"You stole all the merchandise from my store and now you have the nerve to be all calm and smug about it? Just shut up and explain what gives you the right to steal!"

"I'm so sorry, but I had to."

"Why?"

"You didn't take care of their health."

"Only a few of the dogs were sick."

"I tried to protect them all."

"You're so shortsighted. They would have eventually been sold to loving homes and been taken care of by their new owners. That's how a pet shop works."

"I know what you did to the ones who were in the shop too long and grew too old to sell."

"You think you know so much. Tell me, what did I do?"

"I saw the receipt from Healthy Labs."

"I didn't do anything illegal."

"Selling them to a lab in a Third World country makes you a criminal."

"Their cancer research saves human lives."

"Be honest now, are you really trying to save lives here, or are you just doing whatever it takes to turn a profit?"

"How dare you ask me such a thing! You are fired, and that's not all, Miss Pink!"

"Deduct the expense of the animals from my paycheck and we'll call it even."

"Don't make me laugh. You haven't worked here a week. It would take you six months to compensate me."

"How much do I owe you?"

"You stole ten thousand dollars' worth, and that is a felony. I'm calling the police." Sally dials 911 and states what is happening. She's told to call 311 because it is not a robbery in progress. She dials but then hangs up, saying, "Screw these stupid people asking me stupid questions." Then she turns back to me. "How long have I known you?

How do I know what you are and aren't capable of? I'm supposed to trust you to pay me back for merchandise that you stole?"

"You'll just have to trust me. I'll come back with the entire amount."

At that moment, a boy walks in carrying his skateboard. He heads to the dog food area. It's the boy who approached me the other day in the park with his timid friend.

"May I help you?" I ask.

Sally whispers, "Shut up, you don't work here. Don't talk to him."

Without looking up, he says, "Sally, I can't find the special food Big Ash eats. It's not here anymore."

"It's been moved. Try over there in front of the bowls."

He walks over to where she's pointing, to the product section I created.

"Oh yeah, here it is." He grabs a large bag of top-quality dry dog food. "My mom will be right in. She's putting money in the meter."

Holding the bag, he looks up and notices me for the first time. Smiling, he says, "Hey, I know you, you're the dog lady from the park."

"And you're the pit bull lover."

"How is he?"

Sally smiles at me as if she's my best friend. She even goes so far as to place her hand on my shoulder. "The two of you know each other?" she asks.

"She owns the adoption agency for dogs," The boy explains to Sally, proudly scanning the store. "This is my mom's store," he tells me. "Hey, what were their names, the pit bull and the little one?"

"Mr. Bull and Athenia."

"Do you guys need food? We have loads, look at all these bags." He hands me several small bags, which I hesitate to take. He looks to Sally. "That's cool, right, Sally?"

"Don't ask me. Ask your mother. See if she wants to lose money."

"Thank you, you're a kind young man, but don't go to the trouble for me. I can buy food with the paycheck that Sally will give me today."

"You work here?"

"I did."

"There's my mom."

The kind-looking redheaded woman I recognize from the café walks in, smiling like a proud owner. From the corner of my eye, I see Sally spin around, pretending she didn't see her boss and fleeing like a criminal to the storage area.

The boy runs up to his mother. "Mom, this is the dog lady from the park."

Nodding, she says, "Oh, hello. My son mentioned you and the pit bull. Is he still looking for a home?"

"Yes. And there are so many others who need homes."

"Mom, give her some food and toys for her dogs."

"How many dogs do you have?"

"Eighteen are in my room now."

"That's a lot to feed. I need to ask Sally first. I'm sure she won't mind."

"Mom, we should start a peace corps for animals."

"I know, darling. Where is Sally?"

"In the back," I answer.

"My name is Barbara. And that's my son, Lorne, whom you've met. May I ask what your name is?" she says, noticing the pink pants I picked up on 72nd Street. I haven't had a chance to take in or hem the pants. They hang a bit loose and long, but they are clean, and the linen is of the highest quality.

"My name is Miss Pink."

"Somehow, that doesn't surprise me. Lovely name."

"Thank you, dear."

Barbara calls out to the storeroom, "Sally! Sally, I'm here!"

Sally immediately comes out to greet her, carrying a beagle pup in each hand. "Barbara, I didn't realize you were here. I'm so busy. We just received a new shipment of wonderful beagle pups."

Looking at the pups, Barbara says. "They're very cute, but you need to buy more animals. There are none in the cages."

"I know. Something terrible happened last night. She stole them all while I was away. Imagine, I trust her to command the shop and that's what I get."

"Who?" Barbara says, perplexed.

Sally points to me.

"Is that true? But why?" Lorne asks me.

"What exactly happened? Explain from the beginning," Barbara demands.

Sally explains her version. We all listen, including Mrs. Wolf, who watches everything from afar.

"Now tell me your version," Barbara says to me.

"Sally thinks buying sick animals from puppy mills is

more profitable for the shop."

"What do you mean?"

"One died here yesterday."

Sally protests, "Are you going to trust this crazy woman? She obviously stole all our puppies to resell them. She's a common thief!"

"Miss Pink, did you take the dogs?"

"Yes."

"Why?"

"Don't listen to her," Sally continues. "I purchase them from a top breeder, Manfred Farms, and because they are near the city I get quicker deliveries. Normally, they're healthy, but I had a bad shipment yesterday, so Miss Pink freaked out and started all this trouble. Bob is making it up to us. It will not affect our bottom line."

Barbara stammers, "Manfred— Manfred Farms? Everyone knows Manfred Farms is a horrible puppy mill!"

"It used to be, but their management changed a while back and that's when I switched to them as a supplier. Their prices are below market, and of course the animals are treated well."

"You promised me that you would never buy from a puppy mill."

"I've kept my word. It is not a mill."

"We need to talk." Barbara nudges Sally toward the back room.

"We *are* talking," Sally says, as if she has nothing to hide.

"In private, please."

"That's not the whole story," I say.

"Oh?" Barbara says, turning her attention back to me.

"Ask her about Healthy Labs."

Sally strides indignantly into the storage area and Barbara follows her, shutting the steel door behind them.

Thinking Mrs. Wolf is a customer, the boy whispers to me so she doesn't overhear, "I told my mom a long time ago not to trust Sally. I once saw her take fifty dollars from the cash register and tell my mom it was ten."

Suddenly, we hear Sally screeching angrily in the back. Barbara's voice rises too.

Their screaming escalates, back and forth.

"Yes, I did ask for profits, but not at the expense of the animals!"

"You have no idea how to run a business!"

"You don't know what is right or wrong!"

"Run your own business and see if I care if you go under! I have a bright future ahead of me! If you listen to that woman out there, you are listening to a fool!"

Sally swings open the storage room door, grabs her purse, and heads to the door.

"I forgive you," I say to her.

"Who the hell are you to forgive me?" she spits back and slams the door behind her.

Barbara, who looks stricken, goes into the employee's bathroom to regain her composure.

Her son stands behind the cash register, taking charge of the store. "May I help you, ma'am?" he asks Mrs. Wolf.

"No, thank you," Mrs. Wolf says, and walks over to me. "We need to sell one of my sparkly best friends," she says.

"Yes, ASAP. Take Cindy, she will dig it up for you."

Noticing that I know this woman, Lorne walks over to us

with a questioning look. Mrs. Wolf tells him that she wants to purchase the pet store. He thinks she's crazy and laughs.

"Laugh all you want, but it's not over until the fat lady sings."

"Who's the fat lady?" he asks.

"My sister-in-law. And though she loves to kvetch, I can assure you she won't be singing anytime soon," Mrs. Wolf deadpans, winking at me. Her joke falls flat on his innocent ears, as does her offer to buy the store.

Barbara emerges from the bathroom, appearing a bit dazed but calmer now.

"Mom, come over here," Lorne says gently.

Mrs. Wolf flashes a confident smile. "Excuse me, I must be going now. Please have six of these rubber toys packed up and delivered to me," she tells him, putting a hundred-dollar bill on the counter. "Keep the change," she adds, and quickly leaves the store as Barbara approaches us.

"How can we resolve this situation," Barbara asks me in a soft voice, "so the store can still operate while we meet the needs of the animals?"

I can tell that Barbara is desperate for help and is asking in all sincerity, so I take a chance with a new idea that has come to me. "Do you two ever watch reality TV?"

Barbara and her son look confused, but he says, "Yeah, I love *Survivor*. And my mom likes *American Idol*. Why, Miss Pink?"

"I could help you to create a competitive reality TV show. Contestants would compete for the Purple Heart award for rescuing and finding homes for the most dogs."

Her son's eyes light up, but Barbara smiles skeptically.

"How do we make money?"

"Sell the shelter dogs," I say.

"But why buy a shelter dog when you can get one for free?"

"Mom, don't you get it? After seeing this show, people will think it's really cool to buy shelter dogs."

"Okay, but it's not easy to produce a TV show, reality or not, and it takes time for people to get used to paying for what they can get for free."

"First we crawl, then we walk, then we run," I say.

"Where would we start?" she asks me.

"During my magazine days, I collected loads of contacts and phone numbers. I used to call advertisers day in and day out, and I was good at talking to them. I could dig up a few of those numbers. Maybe someone will be interested in sponsoring our reality show."

"Wow, Mom, let's do it! All my friends could bring their dogs in, too!"

"What companies would you call?" Barbara asks me.

"Pet food companies, although very few advertised in the fashion magazine I worked at." The idea of inviting Dr. Styler to sit on our board flashes through my mind.

"I'm beginning to feel that this could work. But how do we assemble a camera crew?"

"Your friends can do it. I'm sure they have cameras."

"I have one, too," her son says.

"Yeah, but honey, we aren't professionals."

"He may not be a professional cameraman, but he's enthusiastic, and that's exactly the attitude we need to get something like this off the ground," I say.

"I know, he's a gem. But we need to look at this carefully. My budget is tight," Barbara nervously confesses.

"Can I still keep my job?" I ask.

"Yes, but please return our puppies."

"I will return them and more."

"Good, but what is the plan? We need to speak practically here. Forgive me if I'm a bit skeptical. I've been burned before, and I can't afford to lose another business."

"Mom, you won't."

Barbara touches her son's forehead and tenderly runs her fingers through his hair.

"I'm sorry for being negative. It's just been rough these past few years."

"How about if we throw a benefit and a doggie dinner and give out prizes for various pet contests," I suggest.

I'm overwhelmed by the dream of saving animals and helping this kind woman and her son keep their pet shop running. I'm not sure what will work, but the ideas are flooding in and everything feels possible.

"Don't you two worry. We are all in this together now. We'll find a way."

They hug me in gratitude and I hug them back. Then I put on my ADOPT A DOG sign and exit the shop.

CHAPTER TWELVE

By the time I arrive in Central Park, I see in the short distance Cindy on her knees digging up the hole with a small shovel and Mrs. Wolf surveying all who pass. Most of the strangers walk by, but some decide to hang around to watch Cindy dig. Mrs. Wolf orders for them to scram and says, "This is not a *Law & Order* rerun." One lady shouts back, "Who the hell are you to tell me to leave my park? I'm a conservationist! My name is on a plaque at the 79th Street entrance!"

I walk over to them. "Hello, dears. Where are the dogs?"

"At home." Cindy turns and smiles.

"Have they eaten?"

"Not yet."

"They won't starve to death, Miss Pinky, but we all will if Cindy doesn't apply elbow grease."

Cindy responds with frustration, "I don't want to damage whatever we are looking for." Looking at me, Cindy asks in a calmer tone, "By the way, what are we looking for?"

"Let's say it's not larger than a bread box," Mrs. Wolf interjects, trying to be charming but sounding pompous. Mrs. Wolf clasps her hands together in prayer, saying, "You can't live with them and you can't live without them." I'm the only one there who knows what she's talking about.

Cindy nervously notices the gathering crowd and stops digging. I notice the strange brown-haired woman who's staring at us. Recognizing her from the yoga group in the park a couple days ago, I wave and smile, but she doesn't respond. I'm not sure if she sees me, because of the intense glare of her sunglasses.

Cindy whispers, "Should I continue?"

"Never stop in the middle of a task," I say. Cindy continues, then squeezes her hand into the hole. "There's nothing here."

"Dig a little deeper. I lodged it in tightly," I respond.

The brown-haired woman approaches me. "I was looking for you yesterday. You didn't pass by the yoga class."

"I've been so busy with the dogs."

"What are you doing with Ruth Madoff? I thought you were a nice person."

"She's not Ruth Madoff."

"Liar."

"There's Ruth Madoff!" The brown-haired woman screams hysterically to the gathering crowd.

She approaches Mrs. Wolf, stands right in front of her, and hisses, "You're her, aren't you?"

"No. I'm Mrs. Wolf."

The woman studies her specimen carefully from head to toe. "My husband died because of your husband."

"I'm sorry for your troubles, but I had nothing to do with any of it."

"You married the bastard."

Mrs. Wolf says, "My husband is in jail just because he associated with Madoff, my friends and family have all deserted me, and I've been stripped of my worldly possessions. I don't even have cable TV. All because of these witch hunts."

The curious bystanders are fixated on us. They must find us entertaining, because they're gawking at us as if at a trio of unusual street performers.

"Let's not talk about what we can't control. Lets help find loving homes for all the abandoned dogs of New York City," I announce, warming to the audience.

"I'm not interested in your causes," the brown-haired lady says to me, "and I revoke the invitation for you to meet me for a coffee."

"I understand," I reply graciously. She's crazier than I thought.

Several of the other bystanders rapidly click their cell phone cameras at us. Recognizing this moment as a great publicity opportunity, I say to the crowd, "If any of you want to participate in an exciting new reality show, come to Green Pastures Pet Store in the East Village. Did you know that according to the Humane Society six to eight million dogs and cats in the United States are abandoned each year, and in New York City around four thousand are killed by animal control yearly? Our show is about the day in the life of a pet owner, her son, and their employees as they adopt shelter dogs and buy puppies from legitimate breeders. Now wouldn't that be just as fascinating as dancing with the stars, and a whole lot more meaningful?"

"Really? This is weird timing, because I'm pitching reality

shows to Bravo and I'd like to maybe bring this one into the mix. What's the address and cross streets, ma'am?" asks a man of about thirty. His tone is sincere and acquisitive, like that of many young movers and shakers prowling around this city.

"East Fourth and Second Avenue," I answer.

Cindy jumps up from the ground. "Oh, Miss Pink, I've always wanted to star in a reality show!"

"Get back on the ground and dig my friends out of the hole, young lady. There's plenty of reality for all of us," Mrs. Wolf says imperiously to Cindy. This prompts the bystanders to ask more questions, which sets the strange brown-haired woman pacing in agitation.

Cindy quietly digs, but to no avail.

"Let me help." I get down on my knees beside her and then realize she is in the wrong place. I crawl to the right about two feet and see the yellowish rock has been moved. More people are coming over to see what is going on.

"I could swear it was right under there," Mrs. Wolf says as she points to where I originally placed the rock.

"Cindy, please give me the shovel." She scoots over and hands it to me. I dig. It's not the right spot.

"Something is wrong," I say.

"What are you looking for?" the brown-haired woman asks.

"I lost my keys," Mrs. Wolf replies sarcastically.

"I'm calling the police."

"Why do that? You think we're stealing dirt here?" I say to the woman.

She looks at me coldly, with real contempt, which sends

a shiver down my spine.

Like a dog looking for a bone, I dig three holes in quick succession. Nothing. I dig another one about two feet away from the last one. I stick my hand in and I feel cold plastic. I tug it out and put the bag in my pink purse.

"Run," Mrs. Wolf says to me when she sees two beat cops approaching.

"No," I say.

The two young cops ask us what we are doing and who we are. I explain that we buried something personal and we are there to retrieve it. They ask me to open up my purse. I do. They then ask me to open up the plastic bag. I do. When they see the diamonds, their eyebrows lift to their foreheads. To my surprise, they don't immediately grab the bag of jewels. I put the bag back into my purse. They order the crowd to leave the area and order Cindy, Mrs. Wolf, and me to follow them to their car.

"I hope you rot in a kennel!" the crazy brown-haired woman screams at Mrs. Wolf and me.

One by one, we are gently filed into the back of the police car. Just before it's my turn, I look back at the park and see the brown-haired woman snarling at us like a rabid dog who's been too long deprived of food and affection.

The two policemen drive us through crowded streets and we finally reach the police precinct parking lot. They ask us to wait in the car a few minutes as they get out, leaving us alone. The air conditioner is blowing full blast, freezing my arms and legs. Mrs. Wolf is in a sweat, fidgeting with her hair. Cindy starts to cry. I discreetly take out the diamond hoop earrings from the plastic bag and slip them in my pocket. Mrs. Wolf is so wrapped up in her pain she doesn't notice. Cindy is worrying about how her father will react.

"I look horrible," Mrs. Wolf says.

"No, you don't," I try to reassure her. "You have beautiful hair."

"It's falling out. Don't lie."

"If I get arrested, my dad will kill me and then throw me out. I'll be homeless and unable to take care of Lilly," Cindy cries.

"Your fears are getting the best of you. But now that you brought up Athenia, I'm curious about something."

"What?"

"Why did you get rid of that lovely little dog when you love her so much?"

"I had no other choice. I was stuck."

"Stuck?" I ask.

"Pregnant!"

"When are you expecting?" I ask.

"You see, Miss Pinky," Mrs. Wolf interrupts, "she has all the luck."

Cindy's face grows rashy red and a torrent of tears falls on her cheeks.

I gently rub the top of her small hand. She grabs my thumb and kisses it.

"I'm a bad person," she says.

"What happened?" I ask.

"I killed it."

"Why?"

"He threatened to leave me if I didn't. In the recovery room, I kept thinking about Lilly and I realized I punished her for my mistake and that was totally cruel. After, like, forever, they finally released me. I walked into the reception area where Bill was waiting for me. He was so busy yapping on his cell that he didn't get up to hug me. I stood in front of him and he waved at me to stay quiet until he finished his call. It's always the little things that break my world wide open."

"Like the straw that broke the camel's back?" I say.

"Exactly. His lack of compassion made me sick. I puked right there on the carpet. The nurse ran out and took me back to the room to rest again. I cried and cried so much I thought my head was about to explode. When I came back out into reception, he was gone. I told the taxi driver to take me to the address of his apartment, but when we were almost there I told him to take me uptown to my father's address instead."

Mrs. Wolf's eyes are watering. She blinks the tears back rapidly, trying to maintain her composure.

"Why don't you and Athenia live with me?" I propose.

"Thank you, but my dad says it's okay, just as long as I train her." She reaches up to brush a loose hair away from my eyes. "You have beautiful hair, Miss Pink. It looks like that French actress's, Catherine Deneuve's."

"There's plenty of room," I say, ignoring her comment.

"She doesn't take compliments well," Mrs. Wolf says.

"Thank you," I say to Cindy.

Mrs. Wolf then turns to me and says in a reprimanding tone, "Don't put her on the street with you. You'll be thrown out tomorrow if Leroy doesn't get his rent."

"I still have my job at the pet shop," I remind her, "and

God never gives us more than we can handle."

"Bullshit. He's given me far more than I can possibly handle," Mrs. Wolf retorts.

"You are handling more than you want to, but not more than you can handle."

"How would you know?" she protests, starting to tug furiously at her hair.

Both policemen return and climb back into the front seat of the car, leaving their windows slightly open. They are waiting for someone or something, but they don't say what.

"Mrs. Wolf, take a few deep breaths."

"This stress is killing me. Now I have a stomach ache."

"Ladies, please be quiet," one of the policemen orders. Right then, as if on cue, Mrs. Wolf lets out a squeaky gust of sour-smelling wind.

"Holy crap, someone ate the devil!" the other policeman says in disgust. They open their doors.

"I'm sorry," Mrs. Wolf says matter-of-factly.

"Quiet!" they bellow.

After several minutes of dutiful silence in the backseat, the man they were waiting for arrives and escorts us into the building. He instructs us to sit on a wooden bench, and we wait there for what feels like hours, leaning our backs against a cement wall. Our stomachs start to make gargling noises.

"I bet the dogs are hungry, too," I say.

"Poor Lilly," Cindy says.

"My Abby must be miserable."

"Precisely, so one of us has to get back there to take care of them," I say.

We make a democratic decision that Cindy should take care of the animals; Mrs. Wolf and I will take the responsibility for the incident so Cindy can walk free and get back to the rooming house. Mrs. Wolf says she's going to use her own attorney. I ask Cindy to tell Sheila about our situation so that she can find an attorney for me. When Mrs. Wolf is allowed to call her attorney, she is told by his fourth wife that he had a minor stroke and is unable to work.

"Schmuck. He couldn't wait until next week," Mrs. Wolf says coldly.

"Sheila can get legal help for both of us," I assure her.

"I hate working with attorneys I don't know."

"Do what you want."

"What I want doesn't come into the equation. I have no choice these days."

"Yes, you do."

"How?"

"What you feel, what you think, how you treat yourself. You have plenty of choices."

"Easy for you to say—you didn't lose everything."

"Yes, I did.

"But not as much or as quickly as I did."

"What's the difference?"

Cindy interjects, "I can help."

"How?" Mrs. Wolf asks while trying to rub old, stuck mascara from underneath her eyes.

Cindy offers to call her father to see if he'll take our case pro bono, assuming we'll be charged for a crime.

A tall, thin detective in an awkward-fitting suit finally takes us into a windowless room, one at a time, and asks us questions about our identities, families, jobs, and why we were digging in the dirt in Central Park. We deny Cindy's involvement. He lets her leave and officially dismisses her case. A few hours later, he dismisses me as well. He keeps Mrs. Wolf and the diamond necklaces in custody. She doesn't want to be left alone with the detective and begs him to let me stay. He says he'll allow it until her attorney arrives. She refuses to answer any more questions.

Cindy's father finally walks in and introduces himself. He has a kind way about him.

I'm officially dismissed and decide to go back to the pet store to see if Barbara will advance me a few days' pay so I can secure my housing situation. As I walk out of the police precinct building, I notice two camera vans, one for Channel 7 and the other for NY1, parked across the street. Noisy reporters and crowds are waiting for Mrs. Wolf to emerge. I hope I can help Mrs. Wolf in time, before she has to face this mob. I'm not that far from the animal shelter. I must ask Sheila for help.

CHAPTER THIRTEEN

A gust of hot air enters with me through the front doors of the shelter. The first thing I see is Sheila petting a fat, old German shepherd who can barely stand up on all fours. She nods hello and gestures for me to wait two minutes until she is finished.

Sheila gently speaks to a very old, slightly bald-headed woman whose back is bent halfway to the floor from scoliosis. "I can see you love him very much."

"I waited until I couldn't take care of him any longer. My husband is ill and I can barely walk myself. King deserves to be in a loving home."

"I will do my best to find him one. But I have to be honest, it's hard, especially with older dogs."

"Older people, older dogs—it's all the same. Nobody wants us."

"That's not true," I interject.

"If you have money, they'll take your last dollar, but we are on social security. We're good for nothing."

"I like old dogs."

She murmurs, "Take King."

"Okay," I say.

"Just like that?" the old woman asks, so hunched over she's peering at me from beneath her left arm.

"Just like that," I respond.

"Bless you."

"Bless you, too."

King knows what is happening. Although he has difficulty walking, he struts confidently over to my side. He does not rub against my body like most dogs do when I treat them with respect, but stands before me in a dignified fashion. His deep, black eyes look into mine and tell me that there is an invisible force drawing us together. I introduce myself with a curtsy and my knee makes a crackling sound. "Hello, kind sir, my name is Miss Pink."

"I'll see you in a few months, old boy," the old woman mumbles as strings of saliva collect on her lips. "Till death do us part and join us again." He ambles back to her, nudges her face with his nose and parks his head against her chin. They know that their parting is temporary. "Good-bye, King." Her pale blue eyes twitch with tears.

The desk phone rings but Sheila ignores it. "Do you need for me to get you a taxi?" she offers.

The old woman shakes her head no. "Where I'm going we don't need taxis."

Sheila graciously opens the door for this determined stranger who wobbles through it without once looking back at King. King doesn't run after her.

After the door closes behind her, Sheila declares, "What she did is admirable. Many of these older people keep their pets long after they can care for them and the authorities end up having to take them away."

We both turn to the new arrival. His tranquility creates calmness in the reception area. When the overzealous volunteer enters to drop off a folder on Sheila's desk, she looks over and sees King. I glare at her, daring her to comment on his being old and frail and unadoptable, but she seems to know what's good for her and leaves us alone.

"How are you, stranger?" Sheila asks me.

"Couldn't be better, dear. Life has an interesting way of working out. I've come for a poodle pup and I get a King. But I can't take King now. I'll come back for him tomorrow."

"That's called a blessing."

"Wait till I tell you how many blessings have entered my life and what's been happening. You'll never believe it. By the way, I need to borrow eyeliner, powder, and lipstick."

"Why?"

"Mrs. Wolf is going on TV and she thinks she looks horrible. Oh yeah, she also needs a hairbrush. I'll bring it all right back."

Sheila's mouth is wide open and she is pointing to the TV in the reception area. It's tuned to NY1. "Too late. There's your friend, the criminal. Turn the sound higher, please. I've got to hear this."

I turn the volume up. The reporter states that Mrs. Wolf has not been charged with any crime and the jewelry she was digging up in Central Park was surrendered to the FBI. It will in turn be sold at auction to pay back the money stolen by her husband's firm. I put my hand in my pocket and feel the earrings.

Sheila spews, "Imagine the bitch's audacity. In full view of us peasants, she tries to dig up her buried jewels."

When I see Mrs. Wolf trying to cover up her tired, humiliated face with her arms, sweat gushes from my every pore and seeps through my clothes.

"Are you okay?"

I can barely breathe. "Water, please."

Sheila runs across the room to the water cooler, but the large container is empty.

"Christ, I asked her to replace this yesterday!" she shouts.

The overzealous volunteer runs in. "What's wrong?"

"You didn't replace it."

"What didn't I do?"

"Get Miss Pink water, pronto!"

I lie flat on the floor. Sheila sits down next to me and rubs my forehead. King offers his calm, reassuring presence.

"I'll be okay. His scent is bringing me back to life."

The volunteer returns with a paper cup filled with tap water. I take a small sip.

"What is going on?" Sheila asks.

"It's not fair to kick a dog when she's down. Especially one who can barely defend herself. Everyone goes after Mrs. Wolf, but she's helpless now. I can't stand to watch anyone take such abuse."

"We have to pay for our mistakes."

"Some more than others, and some don't pay at all. But it's not for us to judge."

"I guess that's the mature way to look at it. But is it the legal way?"

"Judging others can cause blood clots."

She decides not to engage in this discussion. "Let me get you the poodle pup."

"Tomorrow I'll be back to get fifteen more. Give me the worst cases. I'm starting a no kill at the pet shop."

"Fantastic," she says.

Sheila walks away and King lies next to my feet. A moment later, Sheila returns from the kennel area with the perky pup. "He's much better."

I take the little poodle from her arms. He smells sweetly of baby shampoo.

"You can sell him to a good home," Sheila says.

"Wait until he meets Blacky and Mr. Bull. I'm not so sure about the greyhound, he may be too aloof for him."

"Take this Metro card. I found it in the reception area. You don't need to be walking around in this humidity," Sheila says.

"Sheila, I know you didn't just happen to find it. But I appreciate it. Thank you so very much." I go to hug her but she pulls away.

"I hope you understand, that friend of yours has a dangerous side. No makeup artist in the world could cover up her selfishness and greed."

"She's just misunderstood."

"She's using you."

"I'm so sorry you feel that way."

"I feel sorry for you."

I have no time right now to argue with her.

CHAPTER FOURTEEN

The sweltering subway platform is packed with people waiting for downtown trains. They announce "slight delays" because of a small fire on the third rail somewhere in transit. Holding the poodle pup against my chest, I stand behind the yellow line looking down at the dark, empty track when several large rats run by. Thousands of them live down here in the tunnels. The first time I ever saw one was in the seventies when I first moved here. I was disgusted, but after I lost my apartment and spent many nights on subway station benches watching the trains pass by, I came to realize that they too were merely trying to find their piece of big city living. The rats are shy and rarely come out during rush hour, but today they are bold.

A wide-eyed tourist holding a subway map sees a few long-tailed creatures and screams. People lazily turn around to see what it's about, but see nothing and go about their business.

Finally the train pulls into the station and we all pile in, packing ourselves tighter and tighter like a bunch of sardines into a can as more and more passengers try desperately to fit. An announcement comes over the PA system: "Move away from the door." No one listens. A passenger bellows, "Move away from the door, you animals!" "You're the animal!" another shouts back. They get into an argument, with more name-calling and insults to each other's mothers. The other passengers ignore them. We are all standing nose to nose as the door finally closes. My puppy yelps. I pet his little head.

We all sway and rub against each other as the express train snakes through the tunnel, making very few stops. At least the air conditioning is blowing full blast.

● ● ●

The pet shop is filled with people when I arrive. Barbara walks over. "Hi, Miss Pink. Can you believe this? We've had so much publicity, ever since this lady, Mrs. Wolf, told the press about us. We could help so many homeless animals, if only they were here today. I bought several of these puppies from a pet store a few blocks away. When do you intend to bring back ours?"

"In a few hours, but first I need to pick up Blacky and Mr. Bull and the hound and Mrs. Wolf and pay Leroy."

"Oh, he's so cute," Barbara says, noticing the poodle pup.

"He was one of the lucky ones I took out of here and brought to Sheila at the animal shelter. She gave him medicine and love."

"You've done so much for me. How can I ever repay you?"

I put the poodle back into the cage. He circles around on his little legs and then flops down on top of the newspaper.

"If you could advance me a few days' pay, it would cover my next few weeks of rent."

"Not an issue." She goes to her checkbook and writes out a check.

"I don't have a checking account. Can you pay me cash?"

She hands me several bills. I count them. It is slightly under what I owe Leroy.

"Is it not enough?" she asks.

"No, it's fine. Thank you."

"You look worried. What's wrong?"

"I'm just a tad short."

"How much?"

"An eight-hour day."

She hands me more money and I place it in the small pocket of my pink purse.

"This means a lot. Thank you," I say. "Excuse me, we have much business to attend to."

The next thing I do is put fresh water and food into all the cages. We have a Maltese, a beagle, a pug, and an English bulldog. Then I greet a new customer at the door. He says his name is Bob and he's from Manfred Farms. I remember who he is. He's the one who runs the puppy mill, I tell Barbara. She tells him he's evil, he should be ashamed of himself. He tells her the shop owes him money. At his urging, she checks the computer records of invoices and receivables and discovers that Sally has been stealing money by collecting kickbacks from suppliers. When she stopped paying some of the suppliers, they threatened to expose her. Bob was the first one on the list.

"Now what?" Barbara asks.

"We will work it out," I assure her.

A photojournalist from *People* magazine wants to do an

interview with me. I don't feel like it, but Barbara asks me to do her a favor and grant this request. She says that the more exposure her shop can get, the quicker they can secure cash flow.

"What's your relationship with Mrs. Wolf?" the journalist asks.

"I'll tell you what I told her: Whatever you want to receive in your life you must give first. You are in command of your life. The force of what you give will give back to you."

The journalist looks at me funny, but I'm satisfied with my answer. He persists, "Were you involved with her husband's firm?"

This question strikes me as the funniest thing I've heard in a long time. I burst out in laughter and finally say, "Dear, I haven't had a paycheck in years."

"Who are you? Where do you come from?" he asks, looking more puzzled than ever.

I laugh again. "I'm a volunteer at Animal Care Center. I look for homes for shelter dogs. Sometimes I clean apartments."

"Did you clean for Mrs. Wolf?"

Barbara rescues me from this line of questioning and interjects, "But what do these questions have to do with my pet shop?"

"Back story," he says.

"Miss Pink, you really must go to the bank and the post office. It's getting late."

"Thank you for reminding me."

"Oh, and your friend, what's her address? She bought a few things here and paid for a delivery but never left it." I give her my new address. "We'll FedEx it right away. I've found they're cheaper than messengers. She'll have it shortly."

"Thank you," I say.

She winks at me and I make a beeline for the door. On my way out, the grandmother and grandson I ran into earlier come in to buy a puppy. I welcome them and thank them for coming, and direct them to Barbara before continuing on my way.

CHAPTER FIFTEEN

Leroy stands in front of the rooming house, happily sucking in smoke and nicotine, while saying hello to familiar friendly faces. Some of the people rushing by us I've seen before in the neighborhood. In this area there are several rooming houses that don't allow pets, a mission that gives out daily warm meals, a homeless shelter for battered women, and a hotel called Moonlight, which takes in weekly borders—mostly older male drunks. Two blocks away there are several new condo developments, made entirely of glass, which sell from fifteen hundred to two thousand dollars per square foot, depending on the view and the floor number.

"Hi," I say as I approach Leroy. He smiles and blows out a long puff of smoke. I present him with the thick wad of cash. "Take it."

Looking as if he's never seen money before, he asks, "For what?"

"Rent."

He waves the money away and says, "I wasn't going to throw you out. You have a few more days."

"I can't risk even an hour."

"Trust me, I'll give you more than ample time. I've been in your shoes before," he says gently. I know he is telling me the truth.

"I'm honored that you would be so kind to me."

Shaking his head in humility and blushing a bit, he says, "Thank you, Miss Pink. I'm honored that you are honored. Speaking of honor, the honorable Mrs. Wolf just went upstairs. What a day you all are having. You didn't tell me we have a celebrity in our midst."

"You saw her on TV?"

"CNN."

"How horrible."

"I'd say." Leroy is finished with his cigarette and is studying my face. I feel like he's reading a map. I don't want to smile but I do. He does too. Normally, I can't be around anyone who smokes, but his smoky tobacco scent doesn't bother me.

"She'll get through this. She's strong," I say.

"She looked pretty ragged when she came through the lobby, but it's nothing that a good night's sleep can't cure."

"I agree. Healing begins the moment we stop worrying and start to change what we are worrying about."

"Smart lady, you are."

He places his big, warm hand on my arm. "Let me assist you, Mademoiselle Pink," he says.

I have a clear choice: let him escort me or shrug him off. He is kind to our animals and I haven't been touched by a man in years. A win-win scenario is forming. He doesn't seem surprised when I let him escort me into our shabby but clean lobby. A woman sits alone with her back to us, having an intense discussion about the advantages of living in New York City. Her voice is angry, as if someone is challenging her point. Leroy seems unfazed by this crazy lady talking to herself.

"One advantage is I don't need a car," I say.

"What if you like to drive?" Leroy asks.

"Then I'm at a disadvantage," I respond.

He smiles and says, "I have a car. I keep it in Coney Island. I'll take you out there one day if you'd like."

"One day."

The lady stops her conversation and turns around in our direction. I'm shocked to see it is that brown-haired woman from the park.

"Oh my God," I gasp.

"What's wrong?" Leroy asks anxiously.

"Did she see Mrs. Wolf come in?" I whisper.

"I don't know. With her back to the entrance, maybe not."

"Excuse me." I walk away from him and approach her.

For a moment her eyes are blank and her expression almost catatonic. Then she erupts in laughter and tears form in her eyes. I have never seen such confusion.

Forcing myself to sound normal and upbeat, I say, "Hi. What a pleasant surprise to see you here."

"My niece told me I could find you here."

"Your niece?"

"Yeah, I have family."

"I'm sure you do. Who is your niece?"

"Don't ask such a silly question. You work for her."

I'm taken off guard by this. "Barbara is your niece?"

"No. Sheila is."

"Sheila!" I'm shocked.

"Thanks for inviting me to tea," she says softly.

I feel a cold shiver run down my neck. Does Sheila know her aunt is a stalker?

"I don't remember inviting you, but now that you are here, tea sounds lovely."

"What do you know about lovely?" she asks.

"Lovely is a cool breeze on a hot and humid day."

"It's a carving knife at a Thanksgiving table."

"It's appreciating life no mater what misfortune befalls you."

"It's slitting a turkey's neck."

"It's a hot cup of Earl Grey. Let's go. My treat."

"May I see your apartment first?" she asks.

"Why?"

"Friends invite friends to their homes."

"My bed isn't made."

"I like unmade beds."

"Tomorrow would be better."

"Now."

"I'm sorry. That won't work for me."

"I'm not leaving until you change your mind."

Leroy has been listening in and walks over to us. "Ladies, why don't I take you both for a tea."

"Now that's a lovely idea," I say.

"I don't go anywhere with strange men."

"Thanks anyway, Leroy. We'll go alone."

"Excuse me, ladies. Didn't mean to offend."

Cindy runs down the stairs with Athenia following close behind. She kisses me and Athenia rubs up against my leg. I bend down to pick Athenia up, but she eludes my grasp and runs in tight circles around my legs, wanting for me to chase her as I often do.

"Dogs get more love and attention than humans," the brown-haired woman says.

"This one is almost human," I say.

"Not true. Dogs are nothing like humans," she says.

Cindy is unaware of how uncomfortable I am. Smiling, she says, "She refused to pee outside before, but I think she'll go now."

Athenia walks outside without a leash and pees on the sidewalk. From the corner of my eye, I track Leroy. He is waved out of the lobby by the FedEx man who wants him to sign for a delivery. Leroy reenters the lobby with a package in his hand and Athenia on his heels. He walks behind his heavy wooden desk.

"You should leash her. She almost ran into the street after another dog," Leroy says to Cindy.

"Bad girl," Cindy scolds her.

Athenia looks shamed and confused. I pet her on her back and turn to Cindy. "She doesn't know why you are scolding her."

Cindy apologizes to Athenia and says, "Next time, you stay on the leash until you learn."

"Train an unwanted toddler instead," the brown-haired woman interjects.

"Pardon me, Cindy. This is Sheila's aunt . . . I forgot your name?"

"I never told you. It's Mary."

"Mary, meet Cindy. She also knows your niece."

"Sheila is the best," Cindy says.

Mary bristles at this. "I know. You don't have to tell me."

"Yes, of course." Cindy is clearly wondering if Mary is crazy or just having a bad day.

"Why don't you get Blacky and Mr. Bull and bring them down here for their walk," I suggest to Cindy.

"I just walked them."

"You need to walk them longer. Please, go and get them," I insist. With Cindy I have to spell everything out.

Cindy senses something is wrong but still doesn't quite know what it is. I glance over at the desk, but Leroy is no longer there.

"Now!" I demand.

Cindy hurries toward the stairs as Athenia runs around the lobby one more time. "Athenia, come." Cindy leashes her up, which doesn't make sense since it's the end of Athenia's walk, but Cindy sometimes does things backwards.

It's just Mary and me. I stare at her shaking hands and her rolling eyes. I fear something horrible is happening to her. I can't think of ways to help except to make her feel respected. Where is Leroy? Normally someone is always at the front desk. Leroy appears and hands me a package from the Green Pastures Pet Store. "This just came for Mrs. Wolf. I buzzed up for her to come down and get it. She said she'll be right down." He walks back to the reception desk, paying little attention to Mary.

A wicked smile appears on Mary's face. "Speak of the devil. I came here to apologize to 'Mrs. Wolf.' I've made my peace with what she did. I went to church and prayed and now I'm clean of the past. God has forgiven all."

"She understands. I'll tell her you were here and we'll all go for lunch next week," I tell Mary. "Leroy, please buzz

Mrs. Wolf and tell her I'll bring the package to her."

"You got it."

Mary's attention is fixated on the elevator.

"I never understood my niece's relationship with animals. She doesn't take care of her mother—my sister—the way she takes care of her animals."

Trying to appease her, I say, "Pets aren't for everybody."

"She's not answering," Leroy states from across the room.

Mrs. Wolf gracefully walks down the rickety stairs. She is wearing one of my pink pants suits, which is way too large for her. She never takes the elevator because she prefers the exercise. Abigail limps closely behind. They walk like twin sisters—same strut, same pacing.

Out of the corner of my eye, I see Mary reach in her linen jacket pocket and take out a small, fake, pearl-handled pistol. She aims it at the dog.

"Please put that away, Mary. It's not funny," I reprimand her.

She aims at Abigail's heart but misses and hits her paw. Abigail yelps in pain, and that's when I realize the pistol is no fake.

"Ruth, you ruined my life!" Mary screams.

Abigail falls on her side howling, blood bursting from her paw. I push Mary down on the floor and Leroy holds her there and takes away her gun. Mrs. Wolf is momentarily paralyzed with fear and confusion, but then springs into action and wraps my pink scarf around Abigail's paw. Mrs. Wolf is greenish white and is about to faint. I grab her and rock her like a baby as she holds Abigail. The room is reduced to puddles of red blood and walls of white light.

Mary struggles, trying to push Leroy off. "You beast, you're breaking my ribs!"

"Hold still."

She will not stay still. He has to contort his wrestling holds in many uncomfortable positions. Mary screams, "You broke my wrist!"

Cindy enters the pandemonium with Blacky and Mr. Bull. She drops their leashes and they run to my side. "Are you okay?" she asks, also running over to me.

"We are, but she isn't." Abigail is losing a lot of blood and is in a semiconscious state.

"Oh my God, oh my God, oh my God!" Cindy starts to hyperventilate.

"Call 911," I tell her. She runs to the front desk, dials, describes to the dispatcher the brief facts, and then comes back over to us.

"What can I do?" she asks me.

"Help Leroy hold Mary down."

"Don't touch her. She's rabid," he orders.

Within five minutes, the police and ambulance arrive. The dogs bark furiously and Blacky lunges at the policeman. "No, Blacky," I say. Blacky stops within five inches of his uniform.

The policeman's hand is on his holster, ready for self-defense. He orders, "Take control of them, lady, or I will."

"I'm so sorry. They are harmless." I stare at Blacky and Mr. Bull square in their eyes. "Sit."

The dogs do as I tell them, but they remain shoulder to shoulder, guarding and monitoring the movements in the room, ready to pounce on anyone who would hurt their friend. They emit a low, warning growl when Abigail is sedated and strapped on a stretcher and put into the ambulance.

"It's okay, boys, they're not hurting your friend." The dogs calm down. I ask Cindy to take them back upstairs.

There are tears in her eyes. "It's all my fault. If I had picked up more quickly on your hints, I could have saved Abigail."

"It's okay, Cindy. An angel intervened to save her life. Only her paw got hurt."

Mrs. Wolf is standing there in her bloodstained clothes, anxious to join Abigail in the ambulance. "You think she'll live?"

"Yes. Cindy, take the dogs up now, please."

Cindy grabs their leashes and tries to pull them away. "Don't be difficult. I'm in charge now." The dogs listen and follow her without further resistance.

We are invited to climb into the back of the ambulance. Mrs. Wolf seats herself at Abigail's side and pets her little forehead. Abigail is fast asleep, feeling no pain. "Thank God for sedation," Mrs. Wolf says.

In the distance, we hear Mary screaming, "It's only a dog, you fools, not a human!"

It takes two men to hold her and one to handcuff her before hauling her to a police car.

Leroy waves good-bye to us with concern knitted in his brow. I wave back.

The ambulance rushes up First Avenue to the animal hospital. After Abigail's surgery, she recovers well "for an old broad," as the vet puts it. "Not funny," Mrs. Wolf responds. When Mrs. Wolf goes in to see Abigail and finds her sitting up in a cage with an IV in her neck, she calls the vet a "sadist" and other nasty names, though she's deeply relieved to find her beloved girl wagging her tail. Abigail still trusts everyone.

We sit in the hospital waiting room for twenty-four hours, not showering, eating, or speaking to each other. Finally, Mrs. Wolf decides that Mary was temporarily insane and should be forgiven. She also agrees with me that Mary's missed shot must have been guided by the hand of an angel, even though she's not sure angels exist. If they do, she hopes they will come back to save her from losing what little dignity she has left. I suggest that she begin by behaving like an angel herself, by helping others who can't help themselves.

"I'm not a social worker. But I can offer other services, like fundraising."

"That's a great idea," I tell her.

"I'll start with Mary," she tells me. "She had good reason to lose her mind, and it's not like she killed anybody."

Mrs. Wolf wants to thank the would-be assassin for missing her dog's heart. She calls the police precinct under a false identity and discovers Mary's location. We embark on our pilgrimage to the jail. But when we arrive, the authorities won't let us see her, and we return to the hospital feeling very sorry for the woman. We start to plan for financing her legal defense.

When Abigail is ready to be released, the receptionist presents Mrs. Wolf with the bill. Mrs. Wolf says she has no way of paying, and that they should get in line with the rest and eventually the Feds will settle all claims when they auction off her apartment, which she originally bought for ten million.

At this juncture, I hand Mrs. Wolf the earrings I've been holding for her. She looks momentarily surprised, but then adamantly refuses to accept them. "Keep them safe, Miss Pinky. We'll use them for our new shelter."

"But how will you live?" I ask.

"Believe me, I'm more alive than ever," she informs me, her face blossoming into a full smile. She suddenly looks ten years younger.

With Abigail in her arms, Mrs. Wolf and I walk out of the reception area of the hospital onto the sidewalk where taxis are waiting in single file. We find Sheila standing there with her arms crossed over her chest.

"Hi, dear. I didn't expect you to come here," I say to her. "That is so kind of you."

Without responding to me, Sheila steps up to Mrs. Wolf and slaps her hard on the cheek. Mrs. Wolf doesn't flinch. "If your husband hadn't been so greedy, my aunt wouldn't have lost her husband and none of this would have happened."

Mrs. Wolf's stern eyes are concentrated on Sheila's quivering lips.

"Mrs. Wolf refuses to press charges. She knows Mary wasn't in her right mind," I explain gently, but I'm disappointed in Sheila's hardness.

"No one is talking to you, Miss Pink. Stay out of it, unless you want to suffer too."

"Sheila, don't say such hurtful things. I know you don't mean them."

"You are so clueless. Life isn't as simple as you make it."

"It is."

"No, it's filled with greedy, shitty people like your friend."

"Sheila, she is a good soul, both forgiving of others and deserving of forgiveness herself. And she cares for animals the way we do."

Glaring at me while jabbing her finger at Mrs. Wolf's face, Sheila spits out, "As long as you're hanging out with her, don't come near me."

"She's trying to help everyone, even your aunt. Did you know she went to visit your Aunt Mary at the facility earlier today?"

"What are you talking about?"

"Tell her," I say to Mrs. Wolf.

"Why would you do something like that?" Sheila asks Mrs. Wolf incredulously.

"I like abuse," Mrs. Wolf says with a wink, pretending that everything is okay and that she can take Sheila's disrespect in stride.

Sheila looks at each of us for a moment, trying to sort out what we are telling her. Then her expression softens. "I'm so sorry, Miss Pink."

"We all are, dear. All is forgiven."

Sheila turns to Mrs. Wolf and asks, "Including my aunt?"

"Yes," Mrs. Wolf says.

"You dropped the charges?"

"We all have our moments. I understood hers. Now I'm intending to understand yours. And tomorrow I'll understand my own a little better. And perhaps I'll get so good at this that I'll be able to help all those poor animals at the shelter whose hearts are bigger than their bites. Isn't that right, Miss Pinky?"

"I couldn't have said it better myself, Mrs. Wolf. Now, we've all got important business to take care of."

"Oh taxi!" Mrs. Wolf calls out imperiously, as if she's on her way to Saks Fifth Avenue.

"I'm coming with you two," Sheila says.

"Lovely, dear," I say.

A taxi quickly pulls up to the curb, and we all pile in.

"Where to?" the driver asks.

Sheila and I simultaneously tell him the address of the animal center. She looks at me for a moment and then hugs me with tenderness. It feels as good and reassuring as a hug from Blacky or Mr. Bull or Athenia.

Mrs. Wolf opens the window and says matter-of-factly, "You know, New York looks better on some days than on others. Today is one of those good-hair days."

Acknowledgments

Eternal gratitude to my awesome husband, Cosimo, and my brilliant son, Lorne, for their unwavering love and support.

My love and deep thanks to my father, Herbert Louis, and my stepmother, Fran; my two brothers, David and Louis, and my sisters-in-law, Lisa and Beth; my sister-in-law Grace and brother-in-law Johnny; my nephews, Teddy and Anthony; my nieces, Claudia, Stephanie, Madeline, and Alex; my dear Aunt Shirley and Uncle Sol; Uncle Arthur; and my cousins, Sara, Mendi, Barbara, and Wendy.

Last but not least, a heartfelt acknowledgment to the dearly departed whom I think about often: my late beautiful mother, Lillian, who taught me kindness; my late twin brother, Maurice, who taught me forgiveness; my grandmothers, Rose and Ruth, who taught me fashion and to feed squirrels; my Uncle Sol, whom my mother was so proud of; my grandfather Sam, who made me laugh; my late in-laws, Amalia and Giuseppe, who welcomed me with open arms into their home and taught me how to cook.

Thank you, Elizabeth, for all the writing support and endless conversations about my work.

A special thank you to Virginia and Fazia for teaching me to pray and have faith. Yes, you were right—love has no beginning and no end.

A special mention of love for two special souls in heaven: Tyson McRee and Adriano Tassone. You will never be forgotten.

CPSIA information can be obtained at www.ICGtesting.com
Printed in the USA
268049BV00002B/1/P